CREATING NOW

YOUR GUIDE TO CREATIVE THINKING, INSIGHTFUL LIVING AND COMPREHENSIVE SUCCESS

DR. ADRIAN HARRISON

MBBS, FRACP
Chest Physician
Personal Transformation Author
Life Coach
Certified High Performance Coach

Creating Now by Dr. Adrian Harrison

This book is written to provide information and motivation to readers. Its purpose is not to render any type of psychological, legal, or professional advice of any kind. The content is the sole opinion and expression of the author, and not necessarily that of the publisher.

Copyright © 2019 by Dr. Adrian Harrison

All rights reserved. This book or any portion thereof may not be reproduced or transmitted in any form or manner, electronic or mechanical, including photocopying, recording, or by any information storage or retrieval system, without the express written permission of the copyright owner except for the use of brief quotations in a book review or other noncommercial uses permitted by copyright law.

Printed in the United States of America
Library of Congress Control Number: 2019910987
ISBN: Softcover   978-1-64376-286-9
               eBook   978-1-64376-287-6

Republished by: PageTurner, Press and Media LLC
Publication Date: 08/01/2019

To order copies of this book, contact:
PageTurner, Press and Media
Phone: 1-888-447-9651
order@pageturner.us
www.pageturner.us

CONTENTS

Acknowledgements 13
Introduction 15

Part I The Creating Phenomenon

Chapter 1 You Are Creating Now 21
  The Meaning of Life 22
  What Is the Source of Reality? 23
  Understanding Beliefs 24
  Creating the Reality of Your Now 24
  Summary 25
  Practice 25

Chapter 2 The Mechanics of the Mind 27
  Self-Consciousness: The Conscious Mind 27
  Switching Off Our Attention 28
  Subconsciousness: The Subconscious Mind 29
  Two Important Properties of the
  Subconscious Mind 31
  The Relationship Between Self-Consciousness
  and Subconsciousness 31
  Switching on Our Attention 32

	Developing Our Abilities: Training the Conscious and Subconscious Minds 33
	Summary 34
	Practice 35
Chapter 3	**Living in the Now** 36
	The Least Mature Part of Our Minds: The Junior Autopilot 37
	Being Present 39
	Being Present Brings Opportunities 41
	Stay in the Now 42
	Use the Power of Now 43
	Summary 43
	Practice 44
	Reference 46
Chapter 4	**The Creating Process** 47
	The Vibratory Nature of Everything 47
	The Law of Attraction 48
	Create Intentions and Keep Them in Mind 49
	Alignment Between the Conscious and Subconscious Parts of the Mind 50
	Collective Consciousness 51
	Changing the Collective Consciousness 52
	The Power of Vision and Accepting Responsibility 53
	Summary 54
	Practice 55

Part II Upskilling Your Creative Powers

Chapter 5	**Being Intentional** 61
	Attention 61
	Anchored Attention 63
	Free Attention 63
	Maintain Your Focusing Ability 64
	Intention 64

	Expectations 65	
	Use Subconsciousness to Activate	
	Your Attention and Intention 66	
	Direct Your Thoughts and Feelings 66	
	What Are You Focusing on? 68	
	What Is Your Subconscious Mind Telling You? 68	
	Summary 69	
	Practice 70	
	Reference 75	
Chapter 6	**Freedom to Feel 76**	
	Enjoy Being You 77	
	The Depth of Our Emotions 77	
	Emotions and the Quality of Life 78	
	Do You Judge Your Emotions? 79	
	Freedom to Feel 79	
	What Do Our Emotions Tell Us? 80	
	Changing Emotional Step 81	
	The Value of Emotions 82	
	Harnessing the Power of Your Emotions 82	
	Change Yourself Since You Can't Change Others 83	
	If You Want Happiness, Practise Being Happy 85	
	If You Want Love, Develop Your Love Nature 86	
	Summary 87	
	Practice 88	
Chapter 7	**Engaging Imagination 89**	
	Use Your Imagination for Everything 89	
	Roadblocks to Using Imagination 90	
	Freeing Up Your Imagination 91	
	Design Your Life 94	
	Design Your Personality 96	
	Play the Game of Life Differently 96	
	Summary 97	
	Practice 98	
	Reference 101	

Chapter 8	Empowering Beliefs 102
	What and Where Are Our Beliefs?............................ 102
	The Significance of Personal Beliefs 103
	Where to Look to Find Beliefs About Yourself......... 104
	Fears 105
	A Technique to Reveal Beliefs.................................... 109
	Replace Disempowering Beliefs With Ones That Empower You.. 110
	Managing Your Beliefs: Keep a List............................ 112
	Summary 112
	Practice.. 113

Chapter 9	Creating Momentum 115
	The Cause of Procrastination: Some Kind of Benefit 116
	The Cost 116
	The Way Out of Procrastination................................ 117
	Keep Track of What You Are Managing................... 118
	Make Being Organized and Ending Procrastination a Game 119
	Summary 119
	Practice.. 120

Chapter 10	Beyond Your Comfort Zone, Beyond the Familiar 122
	Characteristics of the Comfort Zone 122
	Living Within Our Comfort Zone May Not Be Easy.. 123
	Is It Bad to Live Inside the Comfort Zone?............... 123
	The Pros and Cons.. 124
	Potential Signs of Living Inside Your Comfort Zone.. 124
	Do You Need to Change Anything? 125
	Make a Habit of Challenging Yourself— Explore the Richness of Life....................................... 126
	Don't Charge Into Making Changes 127

     When the Comfort Zone Is Painful 128
     Transitioning from Comfortable to Extraordinary ... 129
     Summary 130
     Practice 131

Chapter 11 Effective Communication 133
     Listening 134
     Listening to Yourself: Mind Chatter 135
     Speaking 139
     Music in Speech 142
     Summary 143
     Practice 144
     Reference 146

Chapter 12 Sidestepping Suffering 147
     Putting an end to Suffering That Isn't Extreme 148
     Eliminate Victim Thinking 149
     Managing More Extreme Suffering 154
     Positive Aspects of Suffering 157
     Is There a Relationship Between Current
     and Past Suffering? 159
     Practice 160
     Summary 160
     Reference 161

Part III Organized for Success

Chapter 13 Systems That Work 165
     Build on Your Successes 165
     Are You Properly Organized? 166
     Roles Help You Keep an Eye on Your Whole Life 167
     See What You Are Managing—Use a Whiteboard 170
     Know When to Delegate and When to Dismiss 171
     Planning Is Essential 172
     Managing Tasks With a Weekly Task List 173
     How to Use a Weekly Task List 173

Use a Monthly Task List Too	174
Organize Your Time	175
Keep a Success Diary	176
Special Memories	176
Summary	177
Practice	178

Chapter 14 Your Ideal Life—The Life of Your Dreams 179
- Breaking Free of a Limiting Reality 179
- Dreams 181
- Dream Your Way Into a New Vision 181
- Keep the Dream Or Vision Alive 183
- Forget About How: Let the Universe
  Manage the Hows 183
- Summary 184
- Practice 185

Chapter 15 Target What You Most Want 188
- Know What You Most Want 188
- The Things About Life That You Value 189
- The Excitement of Goals 192
- Setting Your Goals 193
- Managing Your Goals 198
- Summary 202
- Practice 203
- Reference 204

Part IV Creating Alignment with Your Desires

Chapter 16 Activate Your Mind– Body Connection 207
- The Mind–Body Connection 207
- We Give Priority to Mind Matters 208
- Take Note of Bodily Sensations: They Are Signals.... 208
- Breathing 210
- Look After Your Body 212
- Meditation 212

	Summary	214
	Practice	216
	Reference	217
Chapter 17	**Honing the Power of Your Mind**	**218**
	Thoughts	218
	Thinking	220
	Choose What You Allow Into Your Mind	220
	Use the Power of Transparency	221
	No Worries!	222
	Managing Worry	223
	Managing Your Memory	224
	Create Supports for Your Intentions	225
	Striving Or Forcing?	226
	Identify and Manage Your Problems	226
	Generate More Energy and Drive	230
	Summary	231
	Practice	232
	References	234
Chapter 18	**Be Your Best**	**235**
	Trying	235
	The Difference Between Being and Doing	236
	Being Your Best Versus Being Your Usual	238
	Areas in Which to Practise Being Your Best	239
	What's Your Very Best?	243
	Create the Best in Every Situation	243
	Summary	245
	Practice	246
	Reference	249
Chapter 19	**Don't Let Upsets Hold You Back**	**250**
	The Concept of a "Pain Body"	251
	Upsets Affect Others As Well As Us	252
	Avoiding Creates Resistance	252
	Managing Your Way Out of Upsets	253

	Putting an end to Upsets 258
	Summary 259
	Practice 260
Chapter 20	**Free Yourself From Inner Resistances** **261**
	What Is Resistance? 261
	Being Right 262
	Identifying What We Resist 263
	Move to Higher Ground 264
	Moving Past the Resistance 267
	Moving from Resisting to Finding Solutions 270
	Purpose 271
	Practise Feeling Completely Free of Resistances 275
	Summary 276
	Practice 277
Chapter 21	**Lasting Happiness and Love** **280**
	Don't Tolerate Your Unhelpful Emotions and Behaviours 280
	Managing Unhelpful Emotional Patterns 281
	What Brings You Happiness and Love? 282
	Moving Closer to Consistent Happiness and Love ... 282
	Seven Steps to Happiness and Love 283
	Love and Happiness As States of Being 284
	Are Happiness and Love What You Want? 284
	Manage Your Vibration and Thus Your Connection With Your Higher Self 285
	Summary 286
	Practice 287
Chapter 22	**The Gift of Compassion** **289**
	Compassion 289
	A Practice to Develop Compassion 290
	Compassion Or Judgement: Which Do You Choose? 294
	Taking on Compassion As a Project 295

	Summary 295
	Practice... 296
	Reference 296
Chapter 23	**Quality of Service 297**
	Separation and Connection 297
	Leadership 298
	Continue to Improve Your Creating-Now Ability 299
	New Habits, New Skills.. 300
	Stage-Manage Your Success... 301
	Hone Your Instrument... 302
	The Guidance of Your Higher Self.............................. 303
	The New, Exciting Journey Ahead.............................. 305
	Reconnecting with Your Highest Self Quickly 305
	Summary 306
	Practice... 307

About the Author 309
Bonus Offer for *Creating Now* book readers..................................... 311

ACKNOWLEDGEMENTS

Life is a learning experience, and I have been fortunate to have had many wonderful teachers. Some were important during the first phase of my life, when my consciousness was effective in some ways; but really, it was undifferentiated and undeveloped, compared with where I stand now. My learning journey will never be over, and because of this, the future is a very exciting prospect to me.

To my many teachers, I say thank you. There are too many to name, and if I attempted to acknowledge you all, some would be left out. However, they include my family, my current and past friends, school teachers, university teachers, and especially my personal-development and business teachers. My many medical colleagues and many special patients have also supported and taught me. Through Builders of the Adytum and its Qabalistic teachings, I have "family" who deserve special mention. To all of you, I express immense gratitude for sharing your skill, your love, your time, and your generosity.

To my wife, Donna, I owe so much. By her example, knowledge, beingness, persistence, patience, and love, she has taught and continues to teach me. Thank you, dearest! It is especially to you, and also to all my teachers, that I dedicate this book.

INTRODUCTION

Congratulations on choosing this book. Welcome to *Creating Now!*

Creating and Creativity

Creating and creativity are probably not things most people think about every day. In some quarters, *creating* brings to mind the world of art—artists, musicians, stories, and storytellers—and the sometimes confusing question of what art is and isn't. However, this is but one fragment of the creative world. In reality, creating is a function performed by everyone. It is the process by which we shape our lives and interact with others. Creating is of vital importance to us all. Far from pushing the topic of creating to the back of our minds, we do far better if we make understanding the way we create and make taking the steps to create better our highest priority.

We are always creating. The most important question to ask at any moment in time is, ***"Am I creating consciously, with purpose; or am I creating by default, paying little or no attention to the present or future consequences of what I am thinking, saying, feeling, and doing?"*** Read this short paragraph again, please. It's in bold print so you can locate it again easily: it is that important.

How Well Are You Creating At the Moment?

This book is designed to help you look at how you are creating your life today. It is essential to look critically how you are doing this (ongoingly), because as you are creating today, you are also creating the future. This is a book that shows how to improve your skills and how to consistently create from the highest level to which you aspire. The key to achieving progressively higher levels of clarity, success, performance, wealth, enlightenment, and everything else that you seek from life, lies in the ability you have to manage your mind. Optimizing this ability is exactly what I teach here.

How This Book Will Help You

The journey on which you are about to embark in this book has four parts. These are the sections into which the chapters are arranged. Each section has a different purpose.

- Part 1 builds a foundation for understanding ourselves and how both the mind and the creative process work.

- Part 2 looks at how to improve your creative abilities and how to overcome roadblocks—habitual ways of thinking, feeling, and doing that come at a cost and get in the way of having the life you really want.

- In part 3, we look at several ways of organizing your life and freeing your attention so as to allow you to design your absolutely perfect life.

- Then, in part 4, we pick up more speed and excitement as you learn how to align your body, thoughts, and feelings; and how to eliminate resistances and move easily through problems so that you are free to manifest exactly what you want. You will also learn how to create lasting peace, happiness, and love.

How to Use This Book

In every chapter there are stories, examples, and exercises. The exercises are optional but important. By reading you acquire knowledge. Wisdom results from the deeper learning that comes from putting knowledge into practice. We all think that when we know something and get it at an intellectual level, that's enough. But knowing at an intellectual level truly is the booby prize! Knowing does *not* make a difference. It does not create new habits. A Chinese proverb put it this way: "When you hear something, you will forget it. When you see something, you will remember it. But not until you do something will you understand it." This is why I recommend that you take the time to do at least some of the practices at the end of each chapter.

I also suggest strongly that you don't rush to get to the end of the book. Linger; read the same block of text from one reading session in your next reading session. Make notes. Think about how you operate your mind. How do the comments apply to you? Be aware right from the beginning that your subconscious mind will try its best to sabotage you and stop you from doing these things! It will tell you, for instance, "I know that." Therefore, declare the following intentions right now: "I have taken charge of my mind. I *will* do what it takes to get the absolute most from every chapter. This is going to be fun!"

You will want to read this book again. If someone has lent you his or her copy, you will want your own. This book is a revelation about how we create our lives. It will teach you how to create and live the life of your dreams!

My Invitation

If you are not absolutely convinced this book is for you, here's my invitation, which may surprise you: read the last chapter, chapter 23. Even if you know you want this book, I invite you to read the last chapter. Has any other author suggested such a way-out action to a potential reader? Well, this book is about creating anew. Let's all be prepared to do life differently, more creatively.

Actually, it's very sensible before you see a movie, to watch the trailer or, if you have it on DVD, to watch the last five minutes. You will quickly realize that this is the most effective way to decide if you want to spend the next couple of hours of your life on that film. That's why I'm suggesting that you read my last chapter. I'm confident you will get a definite sense that this book will deliver *all* the benefits that you are demanding from this "mind manual," this ultimate guide to managing your mind and your life.

PART I

THE CREATING PHENOMENON

CHAPTER 1
YOU ARE CREATING NOW

> Everyone's conception of reality is
> capable of infinite expansion.
> —Ann Davies

In the Introduction, the point was made that you and I are always creating. The present moment, then, is an opportunity. You can be intentional, aiming to achieve what you want, or you can allow the opposite—creating in this moment without any specific intention. What you are thinking, feeling, and doing now—either on purpose or without purpose—influences the creation of future "now" moments. As you continue reading this book, you are accepting the opportunity to learn, grow, and create future "nows" that directly and accurately reflect what you want.

Our wants and desires don't occur by chance. They arise from the complex interaction between the world around us and the mechanics of the mind—how we interpret what is present before us and perceive ways it could be improved. Our perceptions and interpretations are greatly influenced by the meaning we give to life. This, then, is where we should start to examine how we create.

The Meaning of Life

Many people struggle and eventually give up making an effort because they cannot find anything worthwhile in their lives. In effect, they cannot find the answer to the question that has been asked in every generation: "What is the meaning of life?" To many people, life seems so chaotic, so random, so purposeless.

There *is* an answer to this important question, and it is very revealing to those who are open to its significance:

> "Life has no particular meaning. You bring meaning to life!"

There is a corollary to this. The source of satisfaction and happiness is not what life gives you; it's what you give to life. So the real question is, "How do I bring meaning to my life?" And the answer to that is this:

> "You bring meaning, satisfaction, and happiness to your life by living a life of purpose—by living each day, deliberately."

This is the exact opposite of living "in reaction," which is the automatic-pilot way in which many people exist. To some extent, all of us tend to react to circumstances. Take, for instance, the international economic downturn that started in 2008 and turned particularly nasty when subprime mortgages and other malpractices led to financial disasters in Greece, Spain, and Cyprus. This threatened the European community and the United States. Flow-on effects occurred all around the world. Governments, large corporations, private companies, and individuals all over the planet found themselves in financial difficulty. At times like these, it may feel like circumstances have a life of their own—circumstances dominate our lives. At times like these, people suffer, and the quality of their lives changes enormously, sometimes forever. Not surprisingly, sadness can be a prominent response. Yet there are others whose lives are equally affected by these same circumstances but who remain cheerful and positive and continue to believe that life is good.

Why do the same circumstances result in completely different realities for different people? Before I answer that, I want to ask another question: What is the source of reality?

What Is the Source of Reality?

The short answer to this question is that reality is always an interpretation of circumstances. The reality we perceive depends entirely on how we interpret circumstances, or expressed slightly differently, the reality we experience depends on the meaning we give to circumstances. Beliefs are important here because they are the yardsticks with which we make judgements or interpretations. These, in turn, lead to the meaning we give to the circumstances we experience.

However, both interpretations and beliefs are thoughts. Through repetition or through their acceptance by notable people, communities, or even nations, beliefs become deeply embedded in personal consciousness. Most of our beliefs are held in the memory of the subconscious mind.

Beliefs shape our realities. As an oversimplified example, the person who believes that something will always go wrong will experience this phenomenon repeatedly; it is a feature of the reality they keep creating. Have you noticed people who always have drama in progress? Then there are those whose lives are drama free. A couple I know always has a new drama to report. Because of their unspoken (and probably unrecognized) belief that something is always wrong, their main focus is on exactly that. They never seem happy or excited about life, which is very sad. It isn't my job to change them or the reality they have created, but I'm committed to modelling something different. I don't join in to discuss the dramas, except to help them find positives in those situations. I change the conversation to things I find inspiring or uplifting.

We create our own realities, and the realities we create are based on our beliefs. Our beliefs operate in the background, usually without us being aware of it. Whether we are relaxing, observing, or performing an activity, our system of beliefs is working silently out of sight—outside the awareness of our conscious mind.

Understanding Beliefs

A *belief* can be defined as "the acceptance that something exists or is true, especially … without proof." Thus, beliefs are more like closely held opinions than truths. It is important to distinguish the difference between beliefs and truths. Truths are absolute; they do not permit reinterpretation or change with circumstances. There are relatively few absolute truths.

Beliefs, on the other hand, are more flexible. They can be modified by new knowledge or deeper comprehension. Beliefs can be created.

Creating the Reality of Your Now

Beliefs can be created. This is great news! It means we are never stuck. We never need be frustrated. We never need be victims of circumstances. All we need to do is create a more positive belief than the automatic one that arrives uninvited and causes the unwanted feeling of being stuck or frustrated. Focusing on positives is how to create nows in which you enjoy living the life you actually want.

This is such an important principle to follow. I'll expand on it as we go through this book. However, it appears again in point 6 of the Summary that follows next, and it is the subject of the final exercise in the Practice section of this chapter. Please be sure to do it.

Summary

1. We are always creating—now… now… and now.

2. Beliefs are deeply held thoughts we consider to be true.

3. Change the thought, and you change your reality.

4. Practise changing disempowering thoughts consistently, and life changes enormously!

5. Don't tolerate negative thoughts!

6. From now on, be the guardian—the absolute guardian—of your thoughts. Say to yourself, "*I* am the master and commander of my thought police."

7. What you experience as reality is a combination of circumstances and how you interpret and therefore respond to them. Mostly, you cannot control the circumstances, but you are *always* in charge of your interpretations of, and responses to them.

Practice

Identify an area of life in which you are troubled, are suffering in some way, are feeling stuck, or want something better.

1. What's the belief—the repetitive thought—underlying what you are experiencing? For instance, it could be "I never get [respect, money, love, good opportunities, etc.]" or "I can't find my way out of this mess" or "I don't know how to …"

2. Create a new thought—a new belief—that you could use instead. Make it a thought that results in feeling better about yourself. Choose something like "I am very resourceful, and I [take care of my needs, create great opportunities, etc.]" or "I choose my own reality; I do not surrender to other people's opinions" or "I see every difficulty as a challenge and an opportunity."

3. Refine your new belief. Write it down. Read it out loud twice every morning when you get up and again before you go to sleep at night. Do this regularly, and within a short time, you will be amazed by the positive changes that are occurring.

4. Take on the exercise in the final paragraph of this chapter.

    - Write down the statement "*I* am the master and commander of my thought police."

    - Read it several times every day.

    - Become exactly what that statement says.

CHAPTER 2
THE MECHANICS OF THE MIND

> The mind is everything.
> What you think, you become.
> —Buddha

At the end of the last chapter was the statement "*I am the master and commander of my thought police.*" Perhaps I should explain that the *I* referred to here is your conscious mind. We can think of the human mind as having two parts, each with different functions—self-consciousness and subconsciousness. We will look at them in some detail now. This will give us a good understanding of the mechanics of the mind and how we can train it to work to our best advantage. In a subsequent chapter, we will look in more detail at how our creating ability works.

Self-Consciousness: The Conscious Mind

Human beings differ from other species of animals in many ways. The most important is our ability to direct our attention. We are able to focus on a particular subject, perceive or discriminate between its different components, learn about it, discover useful ways of relating to it, and put all this to use. Education depends on the ability to focus. Self-consciousness is the part of the mind that has this focusing ability. It is the aspect of the mind that makes active choices.

For various reasons, we can't stay focused all the time. During your first days at a new job, I imagine you focused pretty intently and probably went home feeling exhausted, your head spinning with all the information that came at you. Similarly, having a new baby at home requires focused attention, so this can also result in exhaustion. People vary in their abilities to stay focused. However, like any other skill, we can train ourselves to focus longer and more effectively. We focus best on things that really interest us. If there's a life-threatening situation presented to us, we focus intensely on the person showing us how to survive. If we love music, art, mathematics, or a sport, staying focused is no problem while we are engaged in that activity.

Switching Off Our Attention

When our focusing power becomes exhausted, it switches off. I remember occasions, years ago, when I would arrive home after spending long days as a junior doctor sorting out patients' problems, and my wife would start asking me questions or wanting decisions made. My focusing ability was all used up, and I simply couldn't contribute. I couldn't make decisions that, at another time, I would have handled with ease.

This is similar to our muscles—when we exercise, our muscles get tired. But the more we exercise, the more we can do and the longer we can do it. In the same way, we can train our powers of attention for specific subjects and activities. In particular, we can increase our awareness of what we are thinking, saying, and doing. After a certain amount of time, with frequent, consistent repetition, we learn how to do this automatically. At that point, it becomes effortless and easy.

When we don't engage the focusing ability of the conscious mind, it switches off. I'm sure you can recognize people who use their power of attention very little. They drift through their days, not getting much done. They are operating with the subconscious mind in charge, because when the conscious mind switches off, the subconscious mind—our mental autopilot—takes over.

Subconsciousness: The Subconscious Mind

The subconscious mind is just as important to us as the conscious mind. It has absolutely extraordinary abilities, many of which we can only tap into when our conscious mind becomes aware of and uses them. It is more sophisticated and cleverer than any computer.

Subconsciousness manages all our bodily functions. It beats our hearts, digests the food we eat, repairs injuries, and manages every aspect of our bodies, both while we are awake and when we are asleep.

Basic human instinctual drives are also located in and accessed from the subconscious mind.

Another key function of subconsciousness is its ability to store and retrieve information. Subconsciousness is the storehouse for memories of all kinds. It records everything we have ever done, experienced, said, and learned. When we learn, we are transferring information into subconscious memory in such a way that it is accessible. The ability to retrieve stored information is very important. Different techniques exist for improving both learning and remembering. Unfortunately, this is such a big subject that I will have to leave it you to investigate it elsewhere. Spending time on developing your memory and capacity to learn is really worthwhile. If you are interested in learning about memory and the role of the brain you may like to Google the article "How Memory Works" by Richard Mohs.

Because it knows how to associate related ideas, the subconscious mind is the location of personal imagination. The use of imagination has resulted in enormous changes in every century, particularly the last hundred years. Fully engaging your imagination will transform your projects and enrich your whole life.

Subconsciousness is the realm of our habits, both good and bad. We know from experience how much effort is needed to change them. Why this is the case will become evident in a moment.

Many of our thoughts and feelings (emotions) also come from the subconscious mind. The same is true of beliefs.

Another property of the subconscious mind is that it is interested in things staying the same—homeostasis is one of the operating principles of subconsciousness. We all experience mental inertia—the feeling that what we want to do or are doing is hard work. Inner resistance to doing what, to the conscious mind, is the "right thing to do" can sometimes be overwhelming. This subconscious tendency to keep things as they are works against conscious choices we make to change habits that have probably been locked into our subconscious mind for long periods.

The sense of self-hood and the automatic aspects of personality reside in the subconscious mind. It is fortunate that our perceptions of ourselves are handled by the subconscious, automatic part of our mind. Otherwise, we wouldn't know what to expect from day to day about things like our level of confidence, our usual range of mood, or our likes and dislikes, for example. Our conscious mind may know the sort of person we *want* to be, but the subconscious mind holds powerful patterns of thoughts, feelings and behaviours that have been built up over time in response to our experiences. Many authors call this aspect of ourselves "the ego." However, I think this term can be confusing and inaccurate. We will discuss it and some alternative terms that I prefer in the next chapter.

Two Important Properties of the Subconscious Mind

There are two things that are important to know about subconsciousness because they affect our ability to influence this part of our mind.

- *Subconsciousness responds to subtle instruction.* It responds as we want to expectations, to repeated behaviour, and to repeated activities. It doesn't supply what we want in response to direct instruction or demands.

- *Subconsciousness does not distinguish between "I want" and "I do not want."* It responds to the subject of your attention and supplies that. For example, if you want more money, focus on the feeling of having lots of money (i.e. what you want). If you allow your attention to dwell on being unhappy because you don't have enough money (i.e. what you do not want), what you will attract is more of not having enough money.

Please take note of this paragraph; it is a most important key to success.

The Relationship Between Self-Consciousness and Subconsciousness

The ideal nature of this relationship is like the one between a conductor and an orchestra. Self-consciousness—the conscious mind— is the conductor, and subconsciousness is represented by the players of the various instruments. When the conductor treats the members of the orchestra with respect and provides great leadership and wisdom, the relationship between the two parts is highly productive. The more creative and enthusiastic the conductor is in his role, the more the orchestra pays attention and learns.

An orchestra can play together without a conductor—for a time. But eventually, without good leadership, the rhythm and the correct emphasis on particular notes and phrases—the quality of the music—will suffer, and the performance will deteriorate. The same is true for us when we allow the conscious mind to switch off at inappropriate times. The potential for mistakes and for old habits to emerge is very high without the focused attention of the conscious mind. We can see this if we look at what we say and do when we are tired or stressed—for example, people are more likely to eat junk food than they are to prepare a nutritious meal when they are tired.

The correct relationship between the conscious and subconscious minds can also be compared to two people dancing. When dancing, only one person should lead, but both partners are equally responsible. They are a partnership. With the mind, the conscious mind must always lead and provide direction. In this sense, subconsciousness is the servant of the conscious mind. When the dance is perfected, it is impossible for the onlooker to know which is leading; the partners are truly in a dance—the dance of life.

Switching on Our Attention

We can train subconsciousness to alert the conscious mind to "danger." For example, let's say we discover that we habitually get really annoyed when another person gets angry with us or criticizes us. With our conscious minds, we work out better strategies to use in these situations and form the intention to use them whenever we are threatened. In effect, we activate our subconscious radar to alert us to the impending danger and to remember our new strategies. If this all goes according to plan, our new, happy, and relaxed behaviour will result in positive outcomes.

The more intentional we are about operating in this new, improved manner, the more successful we will become. Before we know it, subconsciousness will accept the new behaviour as its normal response. Our old bad habits have been eliminated.

Developing Our Abilities: Training the Conscious and Subconscious Minds

The great thing is that both the conscious and subconscious minds are trainable. When we know how and where to focus our attention, the conscious mind can provide leadership and train subconsciousness. Training starts with identifying (with our conscious minds) what we want—for example, what type of words we want to use and what words are not to be used; which type of thoughts we will allow, what we value, what goals we want to achieve, and so on.

But that's only the beginning. Repeating messages and being consistent in the messages we give are fundamental in training our subconscious minds. It's like training a pet: disciplined, automatic responses can be taught, but not if you confuse the animal (or confuse your subconscious mind) by saying one thing and doing another.

Meditating is extremely valuable as a way to train the awareness and concentrating ability of the conscious mind. However, even experienced meditators find that from time to time their attention drifts away from their point of focus. Over and over again in meditation, the conscious mind has to recognize that its attention has drifted and gently bring it back to the matter on hand. In this way, the subconscious mind is trained, learning from the consistent expectations and behaviour of the conscious mind. Meditation is thus a valuable tool for increasing our ability to remain present in any given situation. I'll be saying more about this in chapter 11.

Developing our creating-now abilities depends on these principles. It relies on the conscious mind staying alert and in charge. Some call this "mindfulness" or "living deliberately." Whatever you call it, it works. With consistent practice, we train the subconscious mind to support our conscious intentions. These two aspects of the mind are then able to work cooperatively together, creating the equivalent of fabulous symphonies in the form of orchestrated, balanced, successful, and wonderfully satisfying lives.

Summary

1. The functions of the conscious and subconscious aspects of the mind are different.

2. We slip between self- and subconsciousness being in charge so easily that we simply don't notice, unless we know how to recognize the difference.

3. The subconscious mind is the source of most of our thoughts, feelings, beliefs and all our memories and habits.

4. The choices we make in life may be made with deliberation by the conscious mind, or we may react from habit if the subconscious mind is at the helm. Mistakes are more likely when we are in autopilot mode.

5. Development of our ability to create more powerfully and positively involves training the conscious mind so that it provides better leadership to the subconscious mind and corrects errors it finds there. Only with repeated, consistent practice can we train the subconscious mind to support our conscious intentions and increase its creativity.

6. Ultimately, we want a balanced, harmonious, reciprocating relationship between the conscious and subconscious parts of the mind, where each listens to the other and where they

work together, not against one another. With training, they *can* produce magnificent results and concert-quality performances.

Practice

1. Go through the various aspects of your life and write down the things you are interested in. For example, you might choose your career, your family, financial freedom, hobbies, or fitness. These are just a few out of many possibilities.

    - Identify and underline which of the interests you selected are contributing to you having a great future. These are things that should easily hold your attention.

    - Notice the ones that you haven't underlined. Are there any that could be harmful to your future? Do you want to do anything about those?

2. What are some of the things you do that are difficult to concentrate on? (Could you be on autopilot when doing these?)

    - Are there any that you should really be alert and focused when doing them?

    - How could you make them more interesting? How could you get yourself to be more interested in them? Make a list and decide which ones to implement. Be creative here.

3. Think about today. Make a list of the occasions when you think you moved from alertness and paying attention to being on autopilot. Repeat this practice every other day for the next two weeks. Write down what you discover.

CHAPTER 3

LIVING IN THE NOW

*Living in the present moment creates
the experience of eternity.*
—Deepak Chopra

At one level, we think that we are living in this moment. Our senses tell us that this is so. On the other hand, if our attention is not focused on the matters of the present moment, we are not living in the now. We are not present. The body is here, but the consciousness is elsewhere. It's almost as if there is something in us that draws our attention and awareness away from the now and into the past or future. In some people, this tendency is so strong that it can put sanity at risk.

To understand why we fluctuate between living in the past, present, and future, we need to return to our discussion in the last chapter about the two aspects of the mind: the conscious mind (or self-consciousness), and the subconscious mind (or subconsciousness). When we do not consciously direct the mind, the subconscious part takes over. When subconsciousness is at the helm, the automatic personality with its automatically generated thoughts and feelings have the highest priority.

The Least Mature Part of Our Minds: The Junior Autopilot

Most people identify themselves with their minds because, as a result of the constant flow of thoughts, the mind definitely seems to be the most intimate, immediate, and tangible aspect of themselves. Eckhart Tolle defines the ego as a sense of self, which is derived from the content and activity of the mind[1]. I like this short, sharp, uncomplicated definition. However, *ego* is a very clinical term. It is succinct, but it gives us only a very partial view of the automatic aspects of human personality. In their book *The Art of Possibility*, Rosamund and Benjamin Zander[2] don't use the term *ego* and instead talk about "the calculating self." However, this term also only describes one aspect of our personalities.

The thoughts, feelings, and behaviours that are usually expressed through our personalities are like the buildings that we can see as we walk down the street. Just as there are many personality types, the buildings we imagine that might represent them have immense diversity. Some people's personalities are like skyscrapers: huge, impressive, and very sophisticated. Other people's personalities seem far less complicated, with happiness and steadfast attitudes towards work and family; they are perhaps more like attractive bungalows with lovely gardens.

What we don't see as we walk down the street is what the basements of these buildings are like, how deep they go, or how many levels there are below ground. Almost everyone has a "basement" in their automatic consciousness where unhelpful and less socially acceptable behaviours and emotions exist. For some people, these are more appropriate for a spoiled, wilful child or an uncommunicative teenager. Some people's subconscious "basements" have automatic responses that are more like those of a frightened animal. These patterns of behaviour may not surface very often, but they can suddenly emerge given the right circumstances—particularly when we are stressed, very tired, or under the influence of alcohol or drugs.

At these times, we say and do things that we realize afterwards are unworthy of us; we regret our emotional outbursts.

The automatic part of our personalities, and the sense of self with which we are familiar, thus has various layers or levels of habitual thoughts, feelings, and behaviours. Many are sophisticated and very appropriate. However, there are other levels that are less mature, parts of ourselves that would benefit considerably from being trained. I collectively call these parts of the subconscious mind that hold less mature and, in some cases, more primitive habits of thinking, feeling, and doing the "junior autopilot." Sometimes I will just call it "Junior." Changing and consciously recreating these personality habits is eminently possible, and we will discuss this in due course.

There are five key characteristics of Junior, the less mature part of our automatic selves. The degree to which they appear in people's personalities is quite variable. I will describe the full-on version, and you can look at how these characteristics show up in your life. These are normal qualities that you can improve. If the following list makes you uncomfortable, you can be sure your junior autopilot has been prodded. Here we go: (1) Junior is obsessed with its self-importance; (2) it wants to be in charge, in control of ourselves and others; (3) it will do almost anything to survive; and (4) it will do almost anything to avoid "now." This last one might seem a bit odd until we realize that now is where Junior's dominance can be displaced by the focused attention of the conscious mind.

The conscious mind is a threat to our junior autopilot for at least two reasons. Firstly, self-consciousness can displace it and take over the role of running the ship. Secondly, the conscious mind may recognize truths that Junior is avoiding. This avoidance results in a fifth, important characteristic of operating in the junior autopilot (subconscious) mode: the less mature parts of our subconscious minds are extremely dysfunctional.

The junior part of the subconscious mind is only interested in the future and the past. It automatically looks back, remembering previous experiences and events, repeating previous judgements, and reactivating emotions linked to them. When not involved with the past, the junior autopilot projects itself into the future. There it can create either worries or thoughts of anticipation—the seeking of fulfilment when certain circumstances have been met. Even when the less mature part of the subconscious mind is involved with the present, the present is interpreted purely through the lens of past realities or future concerns.

When the junior autopilot section of our subconscious mind is active and in charge, our ability to make conscious decisions about what is best for now is very seriously compromised. An example that demonstrates this is given in the next section.

Being Present

When we are present, we are aware and focused on the events happening in the present moment. Self-consciousness is active and in charge at the helm of the mind.

The opposite of this is being on autopilot. In this mode of mental activity, our attention has moved to something other than what is happening in our immediate surroundings, here and now. The thing we have been distracted by may or may not be related to what is happening now. For instance, if we have just been caught doing something that lacked integrity—such as if someone catches us in a lie—we may be experiencing guilt or anxiety. This is the result of our attention moving away from what has happened—the fact that the lie has just been discovered—and instead, focusing on future consequences.

We can see how our junior autopilot fits into this situation. It wants to avoid the present. Its principal concern is its survival, and any automatic worrying reaction comes from this source. We don't like our self-image to be tainted or to be thought badly of by others. We may even lie to try to preserve our self-image. This is an example of the dysfunctional tendency of this part of our subconscious minds.

When we are present, we are able to retain objectivity about what is happening or has just happened and make effective and even creative choices about what to do now. In the example of being caught telling a lie, rather than opening ourselves to worry about consequences, the more effective course of action might well be to accept responsibility and apologize. This decision would be made by the conscious part of our mind, which is able to put our personal values, such as telling the truth, ahead of the dysfunctional autopilot's thoughts and behaviour patterns from the past.

When we Are not Present

The consequences of not being present depend on whether it is part of our usual behaviour, the duration of our distraction, and whether it happens in critical or noncritical circumstances.

Here are some consequences of not being present. Decide which ones apply to you.

- We don't notice beautiful aspects of our environment.

- We don't notice the generous, considerate acts of others.

- We take things for granted; gratitude is absent from our days.

- Opportunities are invisible.

- We don't operate in our best interests; instead we do what is expedient.

- We perceive risks in our interactions with others.

- We do what we can to lessen subconsciously perceived risks by allowing old, dysfunctional habits to express themselves and run our lives.

- We ignore issues and upsets and deaden our reactions to them by surrendering to addictions to things as variable as shopping, smoking, spending, talking, attracting drama, and more.

- We are far more likely to react emotionally than to choose what we say or do when adverse circumstances occur.

Wow, what a huge cost this has on the quality of life.

We all lapse into autopilot mode; it's the way human beings are made. We don't need to judge ourselves for doing it. All we need to do—if we choose and if we are ready—is to aim to do better, so that we notice when we are not present and bring our full attention back online again.

Being Present Brings Opportunities

When you are present, you notice things. Not only that, but you can train yourself to notice more. We are able to stand outside of ourselves in any situation—as impartial observers—and view it from a wider perspective.

Let me use myself as an example. Often, when I am consulting in chest medicine, I start running over time, and the harder I try to catch up by shortening the current appointment, the more complex that person's issues become. Before I know it, I am even further behind time than before.

What's my autopilot focusing on here? It's mesmerized by the consequences of running late. As a result, I slip into many of the typical thought patterns listed in the previous section. No wonder I feel exhausted and stressed when I don't interrupt the autopilot and put my conscious mind in charge.

When I become present again, I have a wider perspective and free attention. I have access to imagination again. Happy once more, I bring humour into the interview. I listen carefully and creatively. I choose what to address. I am more likely to see when the distress people are experiencing is out of proportion to their symptoms. This is an important observation, because often, the health matters that people complain about are symptoms of something else—underlying fears or unhappiness in other areas of their lives. Providing this more holistic service is far more satisfying to me than focusing solely on health issues. I am now in a state of mind where I can contribute to people's quality of life. In other words, by bringing myself back to being present—with my conscious mind in charge—I am able to create new opportunities.

Which state of my mind do you think my clients appreciate more?

Stay in the Now

Let's think about what *now* means.

- *Now* is the only moment we ever have.

- *Now* is the only time when we are able to think, feel, and act.

- *Now* is the only moment when our consciousness exists.

When we are not present, *now* is not available. It is quite astounding to realize that we spend a huge amount of our lives not focusing on the now.

Use the Power of Now

We can see that it is important to stay focused, with the self-conscious mind in charge, because this is the mode in which we see more clearly, have a wider perspective, and have direct access to our intentions, aspirations, and dreams. It is in this operational mode that we are able to still the mind in meditation, to choose rather than react, and to have access to imagination, creativity, and intuition. *Now* is the moment in which we can apply all these positive, powerful aspects of ourselves, grow, and contribute maximally to others.

How can you be more effective at staying present? Item 4 of the Practice section of this chapter contains exercises that will help with this.

Summary

1. Part of the subconscious mind includes deep-seated habits of thinking, feeling, and behaving that are far less mature than we like to consciously admit. This is our junior autopilot. When it is in charge, the past and the future become our focus. Objectivity—the ability to assess our present situation with care—and the ability to consciously direct and use our creative power are lost.

2. Whether we are present or not depends on whether we are consciously focused and paying attention or whether we are on autopilot.

3. Not being focused and present is unavoidable at times, but there is always a cost. The more time we spend being not present—being on autopilot—the bigger the cost.

4. *Now* is the only moment in which we have any power: the past and the future do not exist, so we are not able to have any influence there.

5. *Now* is the only moment in which we can apply all the positive, powerful aspects of ourselves, grow as individuals, and contribute maximally to others.

6. Keep asking yourself, "Am I present?" Make sure you know which part of your mind is in control.

Practice

1. Make a list of situations in which you notice you are not present.

    Do this first, before reading on. Then compare your list with the list of high-risk situations below.

    <u>There is a high risk of not being present</u>

    - when you are stressed, anxious, worried, or preoccupied;

    - when you are experiencing strong emotions;

    - when you are feeling tired or ill;

    - when you are under the influence of drugs, alcohol, and other mind-altering substances;

    - when you are distracted and thus don't have free attention;

    - when you are on autopilot and are unaware of it; and

- when you turn your attention to the past or the future.

2. Write down some of the costs of not being consciously present

    - at work,

    - at home,

    - in relation to your financial situation,

    - in relation to your health and fitness, and

    - in other areas of your life.

3. For each of these situations, write down the things you could or you will change to enable you to stay present.

4. Practise the following ways of staying in, or returning to, the present:

    - Focus on the feelings associated with breathing: the airflow through your nostrils and the rising and falling of your chest and abdomen.

    - Notice sensations present in many other parts of your body.

    - Change your position. Stand up if you are sitting; walk around for a few moments.

    - Form the intention to remain present—aware of what is happening inside your body, aware of emotions you are feeling, and aware of what is happening around you.

Reference

[1] Eckhart Tolle, *The Power of Now* (Novarto, Ca: New World Library, and Vancouver: Namaste Publishing, 2004), 22.

[2] Rosamund and Benjamin Zander, *The Art of Possibility: Transforming Professional and Personal Life* (London, England: Penguin Books Ltd, 2002)

CHAPTER 4

THE CREATING PROCESS

> There are only two ways to live your life.
> One is as though nothing is a miracle.
> The other is as though everything is a miracle.
> —Albert Einstein

It is amazing that we human beings have the ability to create. We live in extraordinary times where the range of our creations and knowledge is increasing at an exponential rate. One of the things that has become clearer is the mechanism by which we create changes in ourselves and in the world around us.

The Vibratory Nature of Everything

The starting point for understanding the process by which we are able to create is Einstein's famous equation, $E = mc^2$. The practical implication of this equation is that subatomic particles have characteristics of both particles (mass) and energy (vibration). This explains the vibratory property of both energy and matter. The vibratory pattern of particles in solids is slower than liquids. In liquids, they vibrate more slowly than gases. We can conclude that, in essence, everything is energy. When I say everything, I mean exactly that, regardless of whether it is perceptible to or is beyond the limits of our senses, our understanding, and our awareness.

At a personal level, our consciousness has a vibratory nature. Brainwave patterns on an EEG show this. The vibrational nature of our consciousness is altered by things like our moods and our levels of attention.

Just as we are continuously immersed in various types of vibration radiating from the sun and in radio waves emanating from local radio stations, we are also living in an unseen "sea" of subconscious mental energy. This links us not only to every other person on the planet but to *everything* on the planet and even to the most distant stars.

Our individual subconsciousness is like a personal inlet in this vast, universal sea of subconscious mental energy. I'll say more about this in a moment.

Fortunately, we are not aware of all the vibrations with which our minds and bodies are in contact. We are blissfully unaware of them and are free to focus our thoughts on matters of our choosing. However, sometimes the energetic resonance of our consciousness is influenced by, or becomes a match to, the thoughts of others, and their ideas reach us through the medium of subconsciousness.

The Law of Attraction

The law of attraction has become a popular concept in recent times. In a nutshell, it says that like attracts like. We've all experienced the law of attraction. Remember days when you've woken up feeling tired and grumpy, and for the rest of the day, nothing goes right? Then there are days when you decide *I feel great; this going to be a great day.* And it is! However, the law of attraction requires more than wishing and hoping. Let's look at what's involved.

Create Intentions and Keep Them in Mind

What we attract depends on our intentions and how much we focus on them. This is the crux of how the law of attraction works. This applies just as much to creating a great day as winning a Nobel prize. I will be talking much more about knowing what you want later. At this point, though, I would say that most people have not made it a habit to keep on deciding what they want as circumstances change through the day. What do you want when you are travelling to work? What do you want while you are shopping? What do you want as you sit in a meeting with work colleagues, at a body corporate meeting, or at a barbeque with your friends? Generally, people are on autopilot for much of the day and for much of their lives: they give no thought to choosing the most effective matters on which to focus their attention, moment by moment, as the day progresses.

Making the law of attraction work for you means regularly deciding what you want, what you intend, and what you expect. A simple starting point is deciding what sort of day you want to have and then putting that intention into action as the day progresses. "Ease and enjoyment" is one of my favourite intentions. When I focus on this as my expectation, that's invariably how the day turns out. Now, there may be problems along the way, but when they arrive, I think to myself, *Remember, "ease and enjoyment."* The more often I bring this to mind, the more successful I am at having the day turn out as I have chosen.

This makes sense when you remember that subconsciousness responds to subtle instruction, not demands. It's like I'm sending a radio signal of expectation into the sea of subconsciousness, attracting circumstances and people that match my vibratory signal.

What's your predominant vibratory signal? How long has it been like this? It takes time to establish a vibratory pattern that attracts love, success, fun, and abundance, but that's exactly what's possible.

Alignment Between the Conscious and Subconscious Parts of the Mind

You may want something, such as a great day, a better-paid job, or a soul mate, but you will have inner conflict if, on another level you are, for instance, worried you won't get it, believe that you don't deserve it, or don't believe it is achievable.

There is another area where alignment is essential. Your wishes need to correspond to your abilities, your values, and the amount of effort you are prepared to invest in achieving them. Results won't simply happen as a result of wishful thinking or affirmations. Everything needs to be in alignment: your intentions, your plan for achieving your goal, your skillset, your dedication, and your ability to persist.

My success in creating great days has only come by observing errors and practising something better. One way of doing this is by letting go of junior-autopilot-centred pride, thereby reducing one source of misalignment. I also practise going with the flow, allowing things to go contrary to my intentions instead of rigidly trying to stay in control. I haven't perfected these abilities, and sometimes I am embarrassed to find I have returned to old habits, because the result then is usually feeling irritable and upset. Perfection may come later; for now, I'm intent on improvement.

Subconsciousness responds to the predominant vibration, and lack of alignment creates a very strong message. On the other hand, a strong intention coupled with a sustained vision of a particular type of outcome will enable you to perform the tasks for every stage along the way to your goal. When you add persistence and perseverance, achieving the goal becomes inevitable. If you look back at past failures, you will find one or more of these elements was missing.

The law of attraction I subscribe to is not something mysterious or weird; the principles we have just considered are common sense.

The main elements are the things you desire, envision, and believe are possible; your emotional vibrations; and the things you think, speak, and do.

The law of attraction is operating now, and you can only use it now. You use it to your advantage by standing in how things are at this moment and deciding what you will do to bring forth the best outcomes going forward.

Collective Consciousness

Consciousness—both self-conscious and subconscious—is fluidic in its behaviour. It isn't solid or fixed. We see this in relation to conscious energy when we are tired. It becomes harder to control our attention and the flow of our thoughts, so we more easily become distracted or start daydreaming. Our attention tends to drift away from the matter we want to focus on.

The existence of human collective (sub)consciousness (or the collective unconscious, as Jung called it originally) is well accepted. Human collective consciousness, in turn, can be thought of as an ocean that is part of the limitless, universal sea of subconscious mental energy. This is analogous to the Pacific Ocean being part of the sea that covers much of the planet. Our personal subconsciousness is intimately connected to and is part of human collective consciousness. Because of the law of attraction and the fact we create vibratory patterns by our habitual thoughts and feelings, we draw to ourselves thoughts, people, and circumstances that are a match to our vibrations.

The collective consciousness linking humanity explains several phenomena that occur when the energies in subconsciousness are magnified by a large number of people having a similar vibration. That energy can grow, influencing others. World Cup fever is one example. Crowd behaviour is another.

It is the interaction between the subconsciousness of individuals that results in us suddenly being aware that someone is watching us. We may then turn and find ourselves looking directly into the eyes of the person looking at us. In a similar way, some people with unusual, powerful psychic abilities are able to tap either into another's personal subconsciousness or into the collective consciousness to discover personal facts or see into the past and the future. Our linkage to human collective consciousness may also explain why old habits we thought had long since disappeared suddenly re-emerge or why thoughts that seem foreign suddenly come to mind.

Changing the Collective Consciousness

A powerful vision about new possibilities is very engaging. The more energy that is put into the process of enrolling people in an idea, and the more that vision applies to us or to those we care about, the more people are likely to become engaged with it. Advertising is an obvious type of engagement process. It is used on a massive scale in national elections of presidents and prime ministers in most Western countries. On a different scale, people join all kinds of charities because of a variety of visions or desires, such as the desire to help people with different disabilities and health conditions, to help animals, to help sporting endeavours, and so on.

A powerful vision for good can be triggered by disastrous events. Things like the atrocities that continue to occur in the Middle East or the shooting down of the Malaysian Airlines plane over the Ukraine in 2014 stir outrage in people all over the world. What will it take to move from outrage at such inhumane acts to a vision that *demands* an end to wars, hostilities, and needless suffering? What would move your consciousness and mine so much that we would be engaged in such an awesome vision?

Is it possible that humanity will take a stand against the suffering of the millions of people without shelter, food, and sanitation and those who have death and despair around day after day? You might like to think about what's in the way of that. What power of vision and what ability to communicate it would be required to achieve an end to the suffering caused by poverty? We need an enormous mind-shift, an enormous change in human collective consciousness, for this to occur.

Maybe this is too hard to contemplate. The point I want to get across is that by our everyday thoughts and feelings, we already influence human collective consciousness. It is worth thinking about what you can do to help move your own consciousness and the collective consciousness in a positive direction that will benefit humanity. Even small improvements, if taken regularly, will make a difference.

The Power of Vision and Accepting Responsibility

Coming back to our own lives, to creating now, can you see how creating the lives we would love to lead is purely a matter of the power and consistency of our individual visions held over time— that, and being in action?

It all comes down to expanding our sense of—no, our commitment to—accepting personal responsibility.

We have a choice. We could continue looking outside ourselves and finding someone, something, or even God to blame. Maybe we only blame others sometimes, when it's obvious that someone has done something to us. We may never know why certain things happen. The why is totally irrelevant. Looking for the why is looking for where to place the blame.

The other choice we have is to look and find where to place our attention now so we can move forward along the path of success, enjoyment, happiness, and satisfaction. Perhaps the best move might be to develop our sense of self-worth; our ability to love, forgive, or give service unconditionally; or our personal management or relationship skills. It is said that we are either moving forward or backwards in life; there is no standing still. Which direction do you want to go?

We all have times when we find ourselves in the midst of negative thoughts, feelings, and behavioural patterns. These are not opportunities for blame or shame. They are opportunities to sharpen our sense of personal responsibility, our integrity, and our commitment to achieving the vision of all that we hold dear. When we do this, the energetic vibrations we are projecting into the collective consciousness are a positive contribution that helps others do the same.

Summary

1. We live in a vibratory universe, and our personal consciousness creates vibratory patterns.

2. Our personal subconsciousness (our subconscious mind) is part of the human collective (sub)consciousness.

3. Our vibratory patterns extend beyond us into the human collective consciousness, and from it, we attract thoughts and ideas. True psychic abilities (as opposed to fake imitations) are the result of being able to tap into the collective consciousness.

4. Take time to choose a vision of possibility for your own future. Give thought to the ways you can contribute to others and to the causes that call to you.

5. Taking responsibility for finding solutions is helped enormously by having a powerful vision of what you want to create. Living in this way carries the seeds for eliminating suffering—your own and others'. You can be a powerful force for change and make valuable contributions to many people.

Practice

A. **Your emotional Vibration**

   1. Over the next few days, keep a diary of your emotional vibrations, such as being

- angry or frustrated;
- apathetic or sad;
- depressed;
- happy;
- contented, relaxed, or "in the flow";
- inspired;
- enthusiastic;
- ecstatic; or
- emotionless or unaware of emotion.

   2. It would be useful to rate the intensity of your emotional experiences on a scale of one (very slight) to ten (overwhelming feeling that completely takes you over).

   3. Make a note also of approximately how long the emotions last.

   4. How frequently do you experience various positive and negative emotions?

5. Look over your record and identify the predominant emotional vibrations for the period.

6. Make a note of any that you want to change.

B. Your thought Vibration

Over the next few days keep a diary of your thoughts.

- Who do you judge? On what criteria do you judge them? (e.g. appearance, speech, behaviour, etc.)

- Who do you blame, and for what?

- Do you know exactly what you want? If not, list at least five things you want to be, do, or have in the next two months. Then observe and make a note of how often you actively and constructively think (or act) on what you want.

- How often do compassion, generosity, and gratitude appear in your thoughts? Make a point of bringing these into play every day for a week. Write down your observations, because they *will* have observable effects.

C. Meditation

Meditating is an excellent way to practise feeling calm and centred. I recommend you just do it and discover the many benefits. If you do not meditate regularly, set aside five minutes every day for the next week. There are many ways to meditate. This section describes one method.

The first step is to get ready. Take care of anything that is urgent ahead of time. If there are things you need to do that you think you might forget, write them down so they are no longer a concern. Switch off your mobile phone, and if it is appropriate, ask others not to disturb you. Visit the bathroom and do anything else that needs to be done so you are not interrupted.

Set your intention to feel safe, centred, and relaxed for the whole period of the meditation. Make a point of dismissing all thoughts about tasks and concerns. Focus on this as the time to start the meditation approaches.

Sit comfortably with your spine straight and feet supported on the floor. A lounge chair, therefore, is not ideal, unless you have enough firm cushions behind your back to keep you erect, not slouched. Closing your eyes is appropriate, as visual stimuli will then not be a factor.

Bring your awareness to your breath, feeling your chest gently expanding and contracting and feeling the air flowing into and out of your nostrils.

After a few moments, bring to mind the purpose of this meditation, the one you have chosen. A great intention to focus on is your oneness with all that is. Put this into your own words. Then simply hold that thought. Have no expectations, no judgements about what the outcome will be. If your attention drifts, gently bring it back to your oneness with all that is. You may experience deep feelings, or you may feel nothing. You might fall asleep. As you are one with all that is, you will not react to any noises that might otherwise seem intrusive. They are part of the all. Nothing disturbs your awareness of the all.

When you are ready to finish, bring your awareness back to your breath, then to the rest of your body, and finally to the sounds of the world. Move your limbs, stretch, and slowly get up. Be grateful for the time you have just given yourself. Set your intention and your desire to do this again the next day.

PART II

UPSKILLING YOUR CREATIVE POWERS

CHAPTER 5
BEING INTENTIONAL

> Intentions are powerful creations. When repeatedly
> combined with our *attention,* these two can change
> our whole experience of life. Used properly,
> intention and attention produce transformation.
> —Adrian Harrison

In chapter 2, we talked about the self-conscious mind, with its ability to focus attention, and the subconscious, memory-storing habit mind. We said that both aspects of the mind can be trained, and when they are, better performance is achieved. In this chapter, we will be dealing with two important topics that mainly involve the conscious part of our minds.

Attention

The principle tool of the conscious mind is attention—the ability to focus. This is the application of the principle of limitation. Were it not for this ability, human beings would never have progressed from being cave dwellers. By focusing attention, people in every age have developed in ever-expanding directions. Specialization is the focusing of attention on a particular area. Using the power of attention enables individuals to develop their own unique talents and to learn additional skills.

Failure to focus has obvious consequences. Think of things that have happened when people haven't focused on things like their education, their appearance, their spouses or partners, their finances, their houses, or their possessions. Not focusing on what's important has consequences that vary according to the area of life and the duration of the habit of not focusing.

I really like Thomas Herold's analogy about attention. He likened the use of attention to watering your garden with a hose. If the hose has holes, water leaks out when the water flows. This results in less water (attention) on the plants (the goals) you intend growing and increases the potential for weeds (distractions and errors) in places where water leaks away[1].

Many people habitually do not pay attention to the things that matter to them. Instead, they allow themselves to be distracted. Some are distracted by the drama and problems they attract. Others are more interested in drinking, partying, eating, shopping, gossiping, watching TV, and so on, than in paying attention and managing what they want from their life.

What you habitually focus on—what you say, think, and do—attracts circumstances consistent with that. What you focus on expands; what you don't focus on disappears.

I am interested in people's success and happiness. I *know* that paying attention to your heartfelt desires is the way to achieve both. Spending your time allowing your attention to leak away in unthinking, unfocussed activities won't get you there.

Anchored Attention

There are times when something happens and, just like iron filings are drawn to a magnet, our attention is drawn to that event to the exclusion of almost everything else. For instance, if you lose your sunglasses on a fiercely hot summer's day or your wallet goes missing, immediately your attention and your emotions are magnetically attracted to the missing item.

When major life events occur—for example, someone close to you gets cancer, you are about to get married, or a key relationship suddenly ends—these are times when people lose the full ability to direct their attention because it is magnetically drawn to and then becomes hooked and anchored to the major event at hand. As a result, we forget to do things. Our overall management skills become compromised when our attention gets hooked and remains anchored.

Free Attention

The opposite of anchored attention is free attention. Your attention is free when you are fully aware and in control of where you place it. When you are in control like this, you can choose to keep your attention focused on one activity until it is successfully completed, or you can move it to another matter once you actively make that decision. When your attention is free, you are able to bring 100 per cent of your focus to what you choose.

So-called multitasking is not all it's cracked up to be. Multitasking carries the risk of errors simply because our attention is not free—it is divided and thus distracted.

The more free attention you have in your life, the more choices you can make; and with each wise choice, you empower yourself and grow. One of the main purposes of life is growth—extending our abilities.

Growing makes you feel alive. It makes sense, then, that happiness is a result of having free attention.

Maintain Your Focusing Ability

You can see how important it is for our powers of attention to be accessible. This is absolutely essential when creative thinking and complex problem-solving are needed. However, watchfulness and creativity are invaluable in daily life, not just when problems arise.

We are either on autopilot or we are alert and watchful. Life drifts when our autopilot is in charge. When our conscious awareness is fully engaged, we are more likely to identify opportunities, make better decisions, be more successful, and enjoy life more. The conscious mind is the most effective director of our powers of attention.

There are many factors that affect our ability to focus. These factors need to be managed, and they can be managed easily, if you put practical systems in place. Several such factors, each followed by recommended actions, are shown in the Practice section at the end of this chapter. However, it's time now to move on to another really important topic.

Intention

Intention is the conscious mind's second tool. We may pay attention, but without coupling this with intention, the results are likely to be disappointing. Intention gives an additional layer of focus that enables us to achieve the goals and outcomes we want.

Do you remember that in chapter 3, I gave the example of selecting ease and enjoyment as my intention for the day? We can do better than this. We can break the day into sections and set an intention for each section. Here are some examples:

- As we walk to our cars, we might set an intention to be alert and helpful to other road users while we are driving.

- While we are walking into meetings (and preferably even before that), we might set our intention to listen carefully, bring others back to relevant items if their attention "leaks," and to finish the meeting on time with our issues successfully handled.

- While we are getting ready for bed, we might set our intention to sleep soundly through the night and awaken refreshed the next morning. However, many people sleep poorly and have a deep expectation that this pattern will continue. In this situation, other interventions (such as hypnosis, not drinking caffeine after five o'clock in the evening, and not doing any screen activities for thirty minutes before bedtime) are required to enable the positive expectation to succeed.

Setting an intention is setting an expectation. You know how expectations work: expectations send suggestions to subconsciousness. Subconsciousness responds to clear suggestions and manifests what you want.

Expectations

Expectations thus have an important use, but unless they are aligned with intentions, they do not reliably predict success. An expectation is a belief about a particular outcome—one that you anticipate will occur in the future. The problem with expectations is that they may lead to upsets. Unmet expectations are one of the three causes of upsets, which are discussed in chapter 19.

Intentions are much more powerful than expectations for two reasons. Firstly, intentions allow for more than one particular outcome. When your intention is not met, the game isn't over— you look for solutions. Secondly, expectations are a product of the subconscious mind, while intentions are conscious creations that are fuelled by the power of commitment and desire.

My recommendation: replace expectations with intentions. Then, extend your intentions by making definite (as opposed to loose, uncertain) agreements with the people who will help bring your intentions to fruition.

Use Subconsciousness to Activate Your Attention and Intention

We all switch off our focused attention sometimes. We need our autopilot to take over while we rest. But as was said in chapter 2, we can train the subconscious mind to switch on conscious attention when we want. We can train it to alert us to the presence of particular circumstances and even specific states of mind. In particular, we can train subconsciousness to alert us when negative thoughts appear. When that happens, we can train the conscious mind to replace the negative thoughts with positive ones.

Direct Your Thoughts and Feelings

We don't need to be victims to our thoughts. We can stay in charge of them, directing them in the way we want. It takes effort to do this, but gradually, it becomes a habit. When this has been achieved, self-consciousness has trained the subconscious mind to automatically generate positive thoughts.

The same is true of our feelings. We can identify the start of negative feelings and nip them in the bud too. In fact, we can replace negative feelings with positive, helpful, compassionate feelings. This is more great news, because it means we don't need to be victims to the way we feel. We can stay in charge of our feelings. This also takes practice—heaps of practice for some people. Some will find it easier than others, but we are all capable of choosing the feelings we experience.

Let me give you an example of how I changed my emotional reaction to certain people getting angry with me. I noticed that when they got angry with me, I felt dejected and disempowered, and this feeling often coloured the rest of my day. Nothing happened to change this until I first set my intention that I was not going to keep on suffering that way. It was obvious that I needed to consciously do something else to lift me out of this habitual response. I chose two thought activities to achieve this. The first was to put my energy into allowing my Higher Self to live through me, rather than letting my usual, subconsciously generated personality live through me. The second practice I implemented was to focus intently on what I call, my three key words—words that I have chosen as my most important values: *purposeful, connected*, and *happy*. These words quickly bring my focus to being the strong and effective person I am committed to being. At the time of writing, I find I still tend to react to people's anger, but I now very quickly turn that reaction off. Now I stay consciously in charge of myself.

Patience is needed in every type of training programme. Persistence is needed too. We have to expect our thoughts and our feelings to get out of control, particularly during the first weeks and months. But even years later, automatic thought and behaviour patterns can re-emerge. What do you do when you fall off a bike? You get on again and keep going. This dogged persistence, this unfailing commitment to success, must be engaged actively right from the start. We need to remind ourselves of it regularly—don't just wait till you fall off.

What Are You Focusing on?

It can be very surprising and revealing to keep a list of what we spend our time doing and thinking. We spend more time than we realize on autopilot. The transition from one mode of consciousness to the other is seamless; no lights flash to notify us of the change.

So much of what we say springs straight out of the subconscious part of our minds. That's not surprising, because it takes more energy to stay focused than it does to be adrift in the sea of familiar, subconscious thoughts and feelings.

Disciplining yourself to keep track of where your attention is placed may be hard work to start with. However, by doing this, you will become more and more familiar with what it feels like to be in each mode of consciousness. After a time, you will be able to catch yourself drifting (or having drifted) into subconscious functioning and bring your conscious mind back online. Exercises to help with this are listed at the end of the chapter.

What Is Your Subconscious Mind Telling You?

We are not separate from any part of life—we are all linked to each other, to the world, and to the stars through the medium of subconscious mental energy. Because of this fact, we can use the events in the world around us as a mirror to discover what our subconscious minds are telling us.

For instance, in my medical practice, I note the attitudes and problems of my clients and look to see if they reflect part of my life. Am I like them in being late to appointments? Worse, do I forget to keep or even make appointments with the people in my life? Am I rude or abrupt, or do I not listen when talking with others? I ask myself this because some of my patients do this with me at times.

When another driver cuts me off, pulling right in front of me, I ask myself, "Am I behaving in that way too? Do I abruptly interrupt others in some way?"

When my wife reacts in a way that surprises me (particularly if it upsets me), rather than reacting, it is worth taking a moment or two to look and see if I am doing the same thing in an area of my life.

Consider that other people's good and bad behaviours are possibly bringing you a message. At the very least, we can use both as a reminder to improve our performance as we interact with others.

Here are a few other things to look at as possible messengers from subconsciousness:

- What are things that surprise you?

- What are the things that upset you?

- What are you missing, not hearing, or not noticing?

- What are your dreams about?

- Which parts of your body are in discomfort?

Summary

1. Train your subconscious mind to switch on self-consciousness when you want to be alerted to particular circumstances or states of mind. The degree of intention you bring to this influences the quality of the message you are sending to subconsciousness.

2. Don't be a victim to your subconscious mind. Pay attention, so you immediately identify negative thoughts and feelings and

nip them in the bud. Replace negative thoughts with positive, helpful words and feelings.

3. Use affirmations to crystallize exactly what you are committed to in various aspects of your life. Say them aloud every week, and live into them.

4. Make a habit of identifying when you are on autopilot. Bring yourself back to being focused, alert, and watchful. The only way to impact the drift of life is to disengage the autopilot and take deliberate charge again and again and again.

5. Keep track of where you place your attention and where it leaks away. Choose whether to give activities and situations all your attention or none.

6. Frequently reinvent what you are doing; this takes you out of autopilot mode. Surprise yourself.

7. Everything you think, feel, say, and do is taking you towards or away from your dreams.

8. Take note of what your subconscious mind is telling you.

    - Use the people and events around you as a mirror, a prompt to review your own behaviours.

    - Notice your emotional reactions; they reflect your beliefs and indicate whether or not you are attuned to your highest values and intentions.

Practice

1. Deliberately choose the thing(s) to which you give your attention and those to which you don't.

Then give either all your attention or none.

- Practise doing this for a day.

- Keep practising it every day until you have made it a habit.

2. <u>Attention</u>

Here are a number of ways to help you maintain your focusing ability—to keep your conscious mind operating at its best. They all involve looking after yourself.

- *Avoid getting overtired.* Look at your week (and weekends) and work out how optimise your sleep. Look at how you can increase your efficiency at work, with your chores at home, and with your family responsibilities.

- *Eat and drink healthily.* Lots of fresh fruit, vegetables, and water are important. Being a vegetarian is ideal, but this doesn't suit everyone. Consider having several meat-free days each week. Eat in moderation, and avoid fried foods. The skin forms Vitamin D when exposed to sunlight; if you are rarely in sunshine, a Vitamin D supplement will help your bones and many aspects of immunity.

- *Don't smoke; consume minimal alcohol.* Both of these are emotional sedatives. Both markedly affect the functioning of the mind, both in the short term and the long term. They also damage your body. Do what it takes to eliminate smoking, and be intentional about drinking minimal or no alcohol.

- *Have a healthy balance between work and play, doing neither in excess.* Take time out when you need it. Make sure rejuvenation is integrated into your lifestyle.

- *Exercise regularly.* Don't be completely sedentary for a single day.

- *Read books that stimulate your interest and expand your mind.*

- *Invent different ways of doing things.* In this way, you are keeping your power of attention in action. You can do simple things like taking a different route to work or to the gym, buying a different product from the supermarket, getting a new recipe for the evening meal, or reinventing your routine. If you are doing the same things now the same way that you were doing last year, it's time for a change.

- *Get to work on everything that's causing you to suffer.* Suffering is distracting. It is common to procrastinate when we suffer. Make a point of identifying your suffering promptly, and do something about it straight away. Suffering is the subject of another chapter, but the solution always involves using your powers of attention to identify the elements of the problem. Then you can get to work on finding solutions. Some time ago I was shocked when I found that I had been putting up with a wart on my hand and an increasingly painful right foot for over a year. I was busy, and I didn't know what to do about either problem. I allowed not knowing to paralyse me. During a casual conversation one day, I learned that I could easily get an over-the-counter product for the wart. I bought it, and the wart was gone two weeks later. About the same time, I arranged an appointment with a podiatrist. He dug a plantar wart (painlessly) from the sole of my foot, and I walked out of his office pain free.

Why had I waited and suffered for over a year? Because I stayed on autopilot. Deep down, I knew I wanted to get rid of both those things, but I didn't put my focusing ability to work on them.

3. <u>Intentions</u>

- What are your key intentions for this week?

- What are your key intentions for this month?

- What are your key intentions for this year?

Schedule the time to work on these. How much time you need will depend on whether you have already set up intentions for each of the time periods listed or whether you will be creating them for the first time.

If you are doing it for the first time, take baby steps; start with what you can manage. You will probably need several sessions. Make sure none exceed thirty minutes in the first instance.

4. <u>Intentional Thoughts and Feelings</u>

Write down in your own words the kind of thoughts and feelings you are committing to. Create a mission statement, a mantra, or an affirmation that encapsulates it. Examples are shown below.

Repeat the statement of intention regularly. For instance, you can do it when you wake up and immediately before going to sleep, or you can do it when you are going to and from work or lunch—whenever there is a change in your activities.

This is the way to imprint really important thoughts into your consciousness, intensifying their creative power by the use of your power of attention—the focusing power of your mind.

Examples

1) You decide you will be more patient and put an end to angry outbursts. For this you might use the following affirmation every morning, every night, and whenever you notice the first hint of impatience: *My mind is focused on success; my heart overflows with love.*

2) You decide you will be free from financial woes. Practice the following affirmation every morning and as soon as you start experiencing thoughts and feelings about lack: *Like a magnet, I attract the universal abundance. I am the giver and receiver of the generous gifts of life.*

5. Identify What You Are Focusing On

Make quick notes about thoughts that jump into your mind as you go through your day. In particular, identify matters that distract you for more than a few moments. Do this as often as you can for one to two days.

At the end of this time, go over your list of uninvited thoughts. Is there a pattern of topics or emotions, such as worry? Are some of these thoughts about matters you haven't handled or written down in your task list? What is your subconscious mind telling you?

> Repeat this practice from time to time—perhaps one day per month.

Reference

[1] Thomas Herold, *The Principles of Successful Manifesting* (eBook, 2012), http://www.dreammanifesto.com/manifest/ manifesting.pdf.

CHAPTER 6
FREEDOM TO FEEL

> You are what you love, not who loves you.
> —from the movie *Adaptation*

In one of the exercises in the Practice section of chapter 4, you were asked to observe your emotions and make notes about them. Emotions are an important part of our vibratory signals. Chapter 4 explained how our thoughts and emotions are far more than just simple personal experiences. Their vibrations extend into the human collective consciousness. They even go beyond that, into the limitless ocean of universal subconsciousness. I am not aware of there being any way of measuring the effects of emotions beyond personal consciousness. However, it seems logical to me that their influence extends beyond the limits of our individual senses.

In this chapter we will look at emotions from a more conventional, personal perspective. I am going to use the words *emotions* and *feelings* interchangeably.

Enjoy Being You

Feeling happy and enjoying being alive is a beautiful experience. There are so many fabulous things in life for which to be grateful. Sometimes we forget that, because we limit ourselves to thinking locally and personally, rather than as members of the most creative species on this amazing planet.

Our emotions are like the spectrum of the rainbow, and they bring colour to what might otherwise be a fairly dreary existence. Our appreciation of colours depends partly on the amount and quality of light reflected by them—factors outside ourselves. It also depends on something within ourselves: our awareness of and receptivity to their beauty. Similarly, with our emotions, we limit the quality of our lives if we fail to be receptive to their quality.

Emotions usually change many times during the day. If happiness is not your usual, most frequent feeling, do something about it. We'll be discussing how in this chapter. Setting the purposeful intention of being happy is a great starting point.

Enjoy your life. Enjoy being you.

The Depth of Our Emotions

People vary in the frequency and intensity with which they experience emotions. I can remember going through long periods of my life with very little awareness of emotions. Sometimes, this worried me—I wondered if something was wrong with me. It was only after I had been reading about personal development and studying Qabalah for several years that I realized that I had changed. I had become more sensitive, more loving, more accepting, and tolerant. My range and depth of feelings had returned.

Many men, and probably many people who have had a traumatic upbringing, develop the habit of suppressing their feelings. They have learned to do so as a result of their beliefs, which in turn are the product of experience. There can be other causes for having limited feelings, probably related to the development of certain parts of the brain, which are affected by things like birth trauma, maternal nutrition, smoking, alcohol, and the use of recreational drugs and medications.

We can choose to suppress or limit our emotions when circumstances make displaying them inappropriate, or when we feel self-conscious about showing our feelings.

At the opposite end of the scale, many people seem to have such intense emotions that they seem overwhelming. They experience what I can only describe as "emotional incontinence." The sights and sounds of this are often not pretty. They include inappropriate, immature hilarity, major outbursts of anger, floods of tears, and so on. To these people, their emotions are a liability, because they can't control them. They have beliefs that lead them to being highly emotional.

Emotions and the Quality of Life

The emotional spectrum is wide. At the lowest end, we have abject depression and total resignation, which reduce the quality of life to such an extent that all motivation is lost. Anger is a movement up the emotional scale, because here, at least, there is a feeling of energy; anger can be extremely motivating. At the other end of the scale, we move into joy, happiness, and bliss. This is the territory where the quality of life is highest.

Life is never static, and this also true of our emotions. Their changing nature is an important contributor to our quality of life. Would we really appreciate happiness if we were perpetually happy? The complexity and variability of emotions from day to day and between different parts of our lives contribute to us in many ways. They alter the tempo of life, and they add freshness and energy. They let us know that we are alive.

Do You Judge Your Emotions?

People vary in the extent to which they sit in judgement of themselves and their emotions. Sometimes, we judge ourselves for being happy, particularly if people close to us are terribly unhappy because of an unexpected disaster. Others, and previously this included me, are in the habit of judging themselves as being worthless if they lash out in anger.

Is this appropriate? You know it isn't. Sitting in judgement of yourself or anyone else is *never* appropriate; it is never helpful, and it is never right. Firstly, we never know the whole picture, even when we think we do. Secondly, being judgemental interferes with learning. Every judgement sends a negative message to the subconscious mind, reinforcing the negative behaviour that led to the judgement; this message attracts more of the same. When we seek to understand that people always do the best they can with what they have at the time, then we are on the road to making progress. This may be what there is to learn when we or people we are with lose emotional control.

Freedom to Feel

There is a difference between feeling our feelings and expressing our feelings. When the conscious part of our minds is in charge, we are present in the moment, and we can choose whether to express our feelings or not. When we are on autopilot, our habit mind determines this, and we know that in this operational mode of the mind, mistakes are much more likely to occur.

Our feelings are valuable. They are an authentic part of us. It is important that we (consciously) give ourselves permission to feel them. Habitually suppressing feelings comes at a cost.

What Do Our Emotions Tell Us?

Our emotions reflect our interpretations or perceptions of circumstances, and they also reflect our expectations. When I wake up on a holiday and find that the sun is shining in a cloudless sky, I interpret this combination of circumstances and the expectation of having time for fun and relaxation positively and feel very happy. When I wake up on the same cloudless sunny day and know that I have back-to-back meetings all morning, starting in an hour's time, my interpretation is likely to be less positive; the expectation (of a hard day's work) dampens my perception of the beautiful day. Well, this could be the case, unless I consciously replace the expectation of hard work with something more empowering, such as the expectation of a day of accomplishing and contributing.

Our emotions can thus be very helpful. When you experience negative feelings like sadness or anger or you just feel flat, you can look at your interpretation of the circumstances and at your expectations to find the source of the negativity. Then you are in a position to find a reason to feel happy and positive. This isn't easy when you are experiencing strong emotions. However, if you are committed to changing your emotional state so you are happier, more caring, and generally nicer than you have been in the past, you *can* achieve exactly this.

Life's challenges don't have to be difficult. If that's the way they seem, you have some work to do.

Changing Emotional Step

Anger, fear, apathy, and resignation are negative emotions. I am not going to discuss them in detail here. However, in chapter 9, fears and fear management are discussed in some detail.

Negative emotions are the result of negative thoughts (and beliefs). Thoughts can be changed and changed quickly. If we are wise and alert, we can use our emotions to identify when we have slipped into negative thoughts. Then we can alter them by choosing positive, happy ones, thus getting back on track and in step with the harmonious nature of life.

Make this a rule for yourself: I do not tolerate negative thoughts.

Immediately replace negative thoughts with positive thoughts. This may involve redirecting your attention to something completely different. The replacement thought doesn't need to have any relationship to the one it is replacing, though it may. Let's look at a couple of examples:

Automatic Thought:

> *I hate getting wet in the rain.* Upon thinking this, I notice my feelings have changed; I feel less energetic, less enthusiastic. *Oops, I just had a negative thought*, I say to myself.

Replacement Thought:

> *I'm looking forward to having lunch with the girls tomorrow.* Immediately, I feel happier.

Automatic Thought:

> *I'm so unhappy; she doesn't love me anymore.* The quote at the start of this chapter relates to this particular thought and

feeling. Many people have these at some time in their lives. Both depend on the underlying belief that we are victims. When we take responsibility and look at what there is to learn from the situation or look for a positive interpretation, something far greater is possible.

Replacement Thought:

I have so much to be grateful for. So-and-so leaving me has opened the possibility of new people and new experiences. Wow, bring it on! This type of thought is aligned with the first part of the quote at the start of this chapter: "You are who you love." You are who you love, what you love, what you stand for in life, and so on. We are not defined by who does or doesn't love us—unless we are victims to circumstances.

You see the pattern? Positive thoughts, positive feelings. Negative thoughts …

The Value of Emotions

We have already decided that emotions are valuable because they provide contrast in our lives and alter our mental energy. However, in the last two sections we learned something else. Because emotions spring from our subconscious mind, they are a window into it. We can learn about the thoughts and beliefs that are there, below our conscious awareness, if we take note of our emotional reactions. In the section that follows, we are going to consider a third, really important aspect of our emotions.

Harnessing the Power of Your Emotions

When do you have most energy? I know I have more energy when I am fit and when I'm not tired. I was thinking about including "when

I'm not stressed," but on second thought, being stressed can give us enormous energy if we are working on an important project and the deadline is imminent. That's not how I usually want to work, however. It may be effective in the short term, but it is destructive as a long-term strategy.

The best way to harness the power of your emotions is to work on what you want, with minimal or no distractions. This makes sense because (a) you have free attention and (b) you are focused on what you want; you have plugged into the power of your desire nature.

The power of our desire natures is enormous. If we can access this, it gives an enormous impetus to our motivation. Difficult or tedious tasks then look much easier and achievable. We have increased our ability to reach the goals that we really want.

Here is a valuable tip: identify what you most want—what you want today, this week, this month, and in your lifetime. Once you have decided on these, make them priority items, because they automatically activate your desire nature. This is the way to harness the power of your emotions.

Change Yourself Since You Can't Change Others

We cannot change others, but it is possible that they may eventually want to change when they notice the less reactive, happier emotions we are expressing. If there are people you want to change, stop focusing your attention on what's wrong with them. Instead, put your attention on the following:

- Start by looking at your own emotional states when you are around them and the underlying thoughts and beliefs you hold about them. When you find yourself judging them, stop. Pretend you don't know them, and manage your thoughts, feelings, and speech accordingly. This requires discipline and practice, but it won't take long before it starts paying off.

- Use all the information in this chapter and other parts of this book to help you stay in emotionally harmonious step around these people. If you "lose it," realize that you are still learning. Keep striving to improve your performance.

- Don't judge other people. Recognize that just like you, they are part of creation, using their consciousness to the best that they know how. As was pointed out earlier in this book, human beings are not provided with an instruction manual about how to best use our consciousness. We are all learning. We all have areas of skill and areas of novice ability. Look to fix your own flaws instead of focusing on theirs.

- Discover what there is to appreciate about other people, particularly those to whom you react with irritation or worse.

- Take time to visualize love descending on and surrounding the people who bother you. Be generous with them and be generous with yourself.

- Identify what it is that you actually want.

    - Are you triggered by others not respecting you? If so, realize that your self-worth is not dependent on whether or not they respect you. Focus on respecting yourself and maintaining your sense of self-worth.

    - Are you experiencing the absence of love in their presence? If this is the case, statements similar to those immediately above apply here as well. Generate love for yourself. Generate compassion for them. In this way, you will feel centred. You are staying true to your values instead of descending to theirs.

- Do you want happy, low-stress surroundings? Make sure you resonate with the desire to have exactly that. Don't resonate with agitation about being in circumstances that are the opposite of what you want. This is what most people do, and by the law of attraction, they attract more of what they don't want.

If You Want Happiness, Practise Being Happy

Feeling happy as we are creating the now is what everyone wants. We may feel happy when we are working on what interests us and when we achieve what we want, but this is by no means a certainty. In fact, misery often accompanies the attainment of great dreams.

Happiness can be fleeting. What then is the secret of staying happy? It is this: don't rely on outer circumstances to determine whether or not you are happy. Changing circumstances are part of life, and if your happiness is hitched to a particular "star," situation, or outcome, your happiness is unlikely to last.

Happiness, then, is not so much a feeling as a state of mind. You (potentially) have total power over your mind. Thus, you can choose to *be* happy consistently. Provided you stay true to this intention, your happiness is assured, regardless of changing circumstances.

Happiness that lasts is the product of the conscious mind. When we rely on circumstances to make us happy, our happiness is a reaction to those circumstances. It is then the product of our subconsciousness mind, and this is an area where our demands have no effect.

If happiness is what you want, then just practise *being* happy: consciously make happiness your mindset. If you practise this conscientiously and reliably, in time, your subconsciousness will understand that this is what you expect, and lo—being happy now becomes effortless because happiness is now who you are!

If You Want Love, Develop Your Love Nature

Mostly, people think of love as an emotion or feeling. It's a feeling that we like. Nothing beats the feeling of being in love.

Love and happiness are fairly closely linked; both can be regarded as emotions or as states of mind. The comments about happiness as a state of mind in the previous section apply equally to love. Thus, when we experience love, we may do so consciously, because we generate it, or unconsciously, as a reaction. The ability to generate the experience of love is a very powerful skill. When you take responsibility for the way you feel and practise experiencing love or happiness at will, it can have a transforming effect on your life. In fact, I would go so far as to say that choosing love and happiness as your resident state of mind and using your will to install them is the most powerful thing anyone can do.

Please give this some thought. It is within your reach. If many people do this, and love and happiness enter the collective consciousness en masse, who knows what is possible?

Now, we haven't finished with the heading of this section, and you may be wondering how you can develop *your* love nature. I recommend activities centred on the things that you deeply love. Take a look: what melts your heart? Would you love to be involved with babies or small children? Does caring for animals, birds, or certain aspects of nature especially call to you? You may develop your love nature by working as a volunteer in a charity, a kindergarten, a homeless mission, a hospital auxiliary, the SPCA, an animal sanctuary, or a zoo. When you focus your time and attention on what melts your heart, you are on your way to having a fully expressed love nature.

Happiness and love are such important topics that we are going to come back to them towards the end of this book and look at a practice that can train the subconscious mind to generate both.

Summary

1. There is a wide, normal range of emotional experiences. Where you are now emotionally is the perfect starting point for moving towards greater love and happiness.

2. Our emotions enhance the quality of our lives.

3. Don't judge your emotions; learn from them. Being judgemental interferes with learning.

4. Give yourself permission to feel your feelings. The suppressing habit limits our ability to feel the good feelings as well as the bad. Our feelings are an authentic part of ourselves.

5. Our emotions reflect our interpretations or perceptions of circumstances, and they also reflect our expectations. By looking at our interpretations and expectations, we can find the source of our negative emotions. This is where we should start if we want to replace negative emotions with new, positive thoughts and feelings.

6. Don't tolerate negative thoughts. Make the effort to replace negative thoughts immediately with positive ones.

7. Our emotional experiences spring from the subconscious mind, and the more positively and gently we direct this, the happier the circumstances and the emotions it will deliver.

8. The best way to harness the power of your emotions is to focus on what you want, with minimal or no distractions.

9. Identifying what you most want, ensuring that this is appropriate and that you act appropriately to achieve it, is a winning strategy. Aiming for what will bring the most good is your starting point.

10. Stability in being happy and loving can only be achieved by choosing to embody happiness and by *being* love in action.

11. Commit to making happiness and love your resident state of mind. Not only will you benefit, but so too will the people in your life and all of humanity.

Practice

1. Review the chapter 4 Practice section; the exercises there are very relevant to this chapter.

2. Check out what you are thinking when negative emotions are triggered:

    - What are your thoughts and beliefs about the people who seem to be triggering your emotion?

    - Are you judging them or yourself? If you are sitting in judgement, regardless of who you are judging, stop doing that. Read and use the thoughts that can replace those judgements in the section above titled "Change Yourself Since You Can't Change Others."

3. Soon after an upset, identify what it is that you actually wanted in the situation where you became upset. Perhaps you wanted your opinion heard or you wanted to feel valued, for example. Then practise resonating with the feeling of having exactly that. Stop resonating with agitation about being in circumstances that are the opposite of what you want.

    Don't just think, *Yes, that seems like a good idea.* I've made the effort to give you something that can change your life. Please, really keep working on this particular practice, because it will make a *huge* difference for you.

CHAPTER 7
ENGAGING IMAGINATION

> Imagination is the beginning of creation.
> You imagine what you desire; you will what you imagine; and at last you create what you will.
> —George Bernard Shaw

> Live out of your imagination, not your history.
> —Stephen Covey

We use our imaginations every day but often without noticing we are doing so. The purpose of this chapter is to bring to your attention the amazing benefits of taking your use of imagination to a much higher level of activity, using it consciously and purposefully every day as you create each now moment. Maximizing your imaginative abilities will transform your experience of life!

Use Your Imagination for Everything

Using your imagination activates your creativity. The more you use your imagination, the more interesting life becomes. Of course, the opposite is also true, so if life has become boringly familiar, take heart—endless possibilities are at hand through the gateway of your own imagination.

When there is an emergency or a really urgent problem that has to be solved, we generally don't have to decide to use our imaginations—we just get on and use them automatically. That's how we should be every day: automatically looking to see how we could do usual activities differently, and how we could make them more interesting and rewarding.

Roadblocks to Using Imagination

There are many factors that limit our imaginations and prevent them from working effectively. Here is the list I came up with. See if you can find others.

1. Laziness ("I can't be bothered.")

2. Not having made it a habit

3. Being resigned to things staying as they are (i.e., having given up)

4. Being too busy

5. Not thinking of looking for new ideas. (Nobody suggested that I use my imagination.)

6. Having anchored attention (discussed in chapter 5) caused by a really strong emotion, such as anger or love.

All these reasons have one thing in common: they are all caused by being on autopilot. Yes, it takes a certain amount of energy and enthusiasm to make it a habit to use your imagination regularly and frequently. In other words, if your conscious mind isn't engaged, it won't occur to you to try new things or find new possibilities.

Freeing Up Your Imagination

There are several things you can do to make it easier to use your imagination. Just sitting down with a blank sheet of paper can be an imagination killer. Here are some ideas. I encourage you to find more; make this a task that you schedule for completion. Then *please* email me and let me know what you have come up with (adrian@SpinDoctor.com).

Act "As If"

- Pretend you are someone else. You might choose a particular hero from history or someone you currently know. Another option would be to pretend you are already an expert in the area in which you want to advance. Do what this person would do, say what he or she would say. Perhaps pretend you are this person for an hour or longer, and then imagine what he or she would do or say about your life, your project, or your problem. Walk around the room, acting out this person advising you. Record or write down what "he or she" said.

- Pretend (to yourself) that you don't know the people in your family and those with whom you work. When you are with them, make a point of taking off the filters of opinion and judgement that you have been using. Listen to their words as if you had not heard them speak before. See them with fresh eyes. Discover anew who they really are, notice what their concerns really say, and let them contribute to you. Open your heart and your mind. This will transform them … and you.

- In his book *Think and Grow Rich*, Napoleon Hill[1] recommended creating a group of highly respected, amazingly successful imaginary advisers and "meeting" regularly with them (in your imagination) about the things you are managing.

- Burt Goldman came up with another variation. He talks about mentally moving to a parallel universe—one in which your alter ego, or "twin self," is already successfully doing what you want to do, having solved all the problems that stood in the way[2]. Sit down with this successful version of you and let him or her show you around, telling you about how he or she solved the problems standing in the way of success. Ask him or her questions. The answers might not give you the exact solution, but it's likely there will be great clues that you can develop and use.

This might seem a bit far-fetched, but don't judge it—just get on and do it. Have these imaginary conversations for the amount of time that suits you: it might be ten minutes or as long as an hour. Have at least one session each week.

Don't just give it a try; decide to take on one of these practices every week for at least a month in the first instance. Schedule a time when you can practise alone and uninterrupted.

Mini "As if" Sessions

Switch into the "as if" mode when you have a few spare minutes, such as when travelling or waiting. Use your imagination on *something*. Having mini-sessions is a great way to get into the habit of using your imagination.

Brainstorming

Brainstorming can be done alone or in a group. Do it at a time when you are feeling fresh. Pick the topic or problem, and give yourself three minutes to come up with as many answers as you can. You are not just looking for the "right" solution or solutions that have a high probability of success. You want as many ideas as possible, listed without judgement. The aim is to bypass the mind's habitual judging behaviour and allow creative ideas to emerge from the subconscious mind. In this way, your imagination is freed up to go to work.

After a period of time—it might be an hour, half a day, or a few days later—come back to the issue or problem and repeat the process. In the space between the brainstorming sessions, your subconscious mind has had the opportunity to work on that particular topic and find other ideas.

From these efforts, you now have many possible answers to the matter under consideration. Again, at a time when you are feeling fresh, go through the ideas and choose the ones that you will now act on. Some ideas may not be solutions in themselves, but they may lead to the best answer to the problem.

An important principle here is not to settle for the first idea that comes into your mind. Yes, that one might be the best, but there may be several equally good solutions that carry additional possible benefits.

Step Back from the Problem

Imagination and creativity work best when our attention is focused but free. Our imagination doesn't work so well at the end of a long day's toil, for instance. If you have been working intensively on a subject for weeks or months and feel stuck, it is time to step back. Make time for relaxation and rejuvenation.

It is important to build R & R time into your schedule, including taking holidays. Don't wait till you are exhausted and need a break. Put arrangements for holidays in place at regular times during the year. Going from problem to problem without let-up is a sure way to kill off your creativity. Persistent toil without R & R doesn't work in the long run as a routine practice. We all have phases of focused concentration that require disciplined persistence in order to achieve a successful outcome. However, if this is the usual pattern of your life, use your imagination—brainstorm solutions and create a new schedule that includes the fun and rejuvenation that are so vital for keeping your creativity at its peak.

Look After All Your Interests and Activities

Know what's important to you and don't ignore the important things in your life. Make sure you manage your health and fitness, because without a well-functioning body, everything else is put at risk. Take care of your relationships as much as your finances and your job. As you manage your life, use your imagination; give priority to bringing happiness and success to all the areas of your life.

Design Your Life

This leads us to the topic of designing your life. Perhaps life has just seemed to evolve. Perhaps you have moved from childhood to adulthood, and life is going well, thank you. If this is you—congratulations. I'm sure you put in effort where it was needed to get you where you are now.

But wait, there's more. There is far more available to all of us than maintaining the status quo. It's not that there is anything wrong with keeping things as they are now, although many people *are* dissatisfied and want more.

When you read the phrase *design your life*, what came to mind? Was it "Oh no, he wants me to do some work!" or something similar? Hey, you couldn't be further from the truth. I want you to have more fun! What would it be like if you were having ten or a hundred times more fun than you have had in the last ten years?

Design your life for happiness, love, fun, freedom, and abundance. They are the only things that matter. You disagree? Well, to me, their opposite is suffering, and while even that has positive aspects, it's not where most people want to aim their presents and their futures.

Now isn't the time when we are going to look in detail at designing your life. You can be at work on this all the time by choosing what you want and where you put your attention. You can schedule time each week or each month to imagine and then choose the directions you want to take your life. Then every week, you can focus on doing what you need to do to get there. We will look at many topics that will help you design your life in chapters 14 and 15.

Let me tell you about a couple, whom I'll call Jason and Carla, who recently redesigned their lives. Both were in their late forties; they had two teenage sons, a dog, and a cat. Jason was a talented freelance software creator earning a modest income from contract work. In the last three years, Carla had tried to set up a boutique clothing business, but the return on her time, money, and effort was small. She was ready to quit. Essential items, education expenses, and mortgage payments were consuming their income; they hadn't had a real holiday in years. They asked for help in redesigning their lives because they felt stuck. They badly wanted life to be more enjoyable and financially rewarding.

On my suggestion, they had a valuation on their home and got advice about what improvements would be worth doing. They also saw a financial adviser. I had them draw up a list of their interests and activities, which included Jason coaching soccer at the local school, their wish to set up a charitable trust to help the children of single parents, their love of adventure travel, and lots more. They also made a list of their skills, strengths, and weaknesses. Then they brainstormed, individually and later together, about how they might use their skills in each area of interest so as to generate a regular income.

The outcome, six months later, was that the family decided to move to Queenstown, in New Zealand's South Island. Jason had discovered a small travel-adventure firm there that needed a partner who would bring new enthusiasm and new skills. Jason's love of fitness, hiking, and other outdoor activities and Carla's organizing and business skills were a perfect match for the company. They had enough capital in their existing home to buy a fairly new home near Lake Hayes. Jason still does some software contract work in his spare time. They are immensely excited about their new lives and the new challenges they have created. And of course they love their fabulous new environment.

Design Your Personality

In the same way that you can design your life, you can design the sort of person you want to be. You are only stuck in the way you are if that's what you believe. Open the possibility of changing yourself by thinking, *I am coming round to the idea of being ...* (you fill in the rest). You might put *a better parent, grandparent, friend,* or *spouse*. What area of your life do you want to improve? Start redesigning your life there. Then use your imagination to create new ways of doing and being.

Values are the qualities we want to express routinely in our thoughts, speech, our behaviour and in what we are doing in life. We may have grown up with habits that are not in keeping with our own deeply held values. Until you discover what your values are, you won't know if you are applying them consistently in your life. We will look at values in much more detail in chapter 15.

If you are not completely satisfied with yourself or aspects of your life, it *is* possible to become a happier person and to be more effective and successful than you currently are. It is possible, desirable, and profitable to design your personality. Once you know what you want, you can use your desire, commitment and imagination to achieve it.

Play the Game of Life Differently

Look at how you are in life. Do you play it small and safe with not much at stake? Do you play it large, energetically, and full-on? There is no right or wrong way to approach living. However, we humans are creatures of habit. Many people tend to operate within their comfort zones. The best way to make life turn out the way you want is to start doing things differently. This doesn't mean making radical changes. In fact, the opposite is far better—start with one thing that is small and manageable and complete that. Then choose the next thing to change. Make sure every step brings success. Keep moving forward like this, making success your intention with every goal.

Have a look at the Practice section of this chapter, because there are practices there that, little by little, can help you to start creating the game of your life.

Summary

1. The more you use your imagination, the more creative and interesting life becomes.

2. Eliminate roadblocks to using your imagination. If you feel unmotivated or stuck, just use your imagination to find solutions—you don't have to suffer.

3. Use your schedule: be creative in scheduling time in which you use your imagination.

4. Make a point of taking every opportunity to engage your imagination; make this your favourite game, and play it many times every day.

5. Make sure you use your imagination to manage your *whole* life, not just your primary interest, such as your job or your children.

6. You are a wonderful designer of your life. Make your life sing with happiness: you are creating now!

Practice

1. Pick an activity that you do frequently and find uninteresting. It might be vacuuming the house, cleaning up after meals, or even preparing meals. Just pick one of these now, unless there is another activity on which you would like to practise using your imagination.

    - Brainstorm thoughts you could have about this activity that don't include things like *it's boring, it's a chore*, or *I wish I didn't have to waste time on this*, and so on. Make sure you pick thoughts that are positive and inspiring.

    - An alternative approach is to pretend you are someone you respect and admire, one of your heroes or heroines. Stand in that person's shoes. What would his or her attitude be to this activity? Why would he or she value it?

2. Pick a problem and brainstorm it every other day. Follow the steps outlined above in the section "Freeing up Your Imagination."

3. Be spontaneous in using your imagination.

    - Take a different route on your next journey.

    - Pick a book to read that wouldn't usually be your first choice.

    - Take on a different personality trait: be Mr. Generosity or Miss Cheerful-in-My-Work, for instance.

    - Create an adventure, and go on it soon.

- Speak to people you wouldn't ordinarily speak to.

4. Invent a new career just because you can.

    - Have a brainstorming session on what you would want to be doing if you were not in your present job or role.

    - Now, imagine you are in your new career, and write a letter or a story describing what you are doing, how you got to be doing it, how it has changed your life, what other benefits have occurred through having this job, and where this job might ultimately lead. Make it up. Make it really interesting. Pretend you are writing it for publication or for a competition.

5. Create one new habit every month, and do it every day for a month. What you choose can be as complicated or as simple as you want. Here are a few suggestions:

    - Choose to not be a worrier.

    - Choose to not buy into other people's issues: do what needs to be done, but be impartial as well as supportive with others.

    - Choose to share responsibilities for housework with the people you live with.

    - Be a contented, happy, and helpful person at work.

    - Take thirty minutes for yourself, perhaps at lunchtime, to enjoy something. It might be to read, to listen to beautiful music, to exercise, or to practise playing a musical instrument.

- Choose not to consume alcohol for a month.

- Decide to meditate every day for the next month.

- Choose something vastly more creative than any of the items on this list.

6. Design your next holiday. Be adventurous. (Note that I said "adventurous," not dangerous.)

7. Write a description of the new you.

- What's the principle activity in which the new you will feature? Start this article about yourself with that information. Hold that activity in mind while you complete your description, knowing also that this new you will be you in every corner of your life.

- Include at least twenty descriptive terms. For example, you might decide to be unstoppable, graceful, a high-flying star, foremost in your field, or Mother Teresa to your flock. Paint a picture that inspires you. Push the boundaries way beyond the present (former) you.

- Read your creation every day and feel the excitement and achievement. Most importantly, live into being the new you now!

- Finally, look for and make a note of what's in the way of you being that new you. Do you need additional skills? Do you need to change jobs? Do you need to clean up any relationships? What's in the way? Perhaps you need to lose weight or become fit for the first time in your life. Find out what's in the way and start dealing with it.

Reference

1   Napoleon Hill, *Think and Grow Rich*. (New York & Toronto: Ballantine Books, 1937)

2   Burt Goldman. http://www.quantumjumping.com/.

CHAPTER 8

EMPOWERING BELIEFS

> Don't believe everything you think.
> —Anonymous

Much has been written about beliefs, and this chapter could be very complex if we were to approach the subject of beliefs from either a philosophical or psychological direction. However, the purpose of this book is to help you to take actions and make progress. It is from this practical perspective that this chapter has been written.

The subject of beliefs was introduced in chapter 1, and it will be really helpful if you go back to read the few short paragraphs on this subject again.

What and Where Are Our Beliefs?

Basically, beliefs are thoughts whose content we understand to contain truth. Depending on the subject and context, there is a wide range of intensity and depth of attachment that we can have to the thoughts we call beliefs. Religious beliefs, beliefs that have been shaped by events that have deeply impacted us during our formative years, and beliefs resulting from words or actions that were repeated many times by those closest to us as we grew up are some of our longest held and most deeply held beliefs.

Just because we regard our beliefs as truths does not mean that they are in fact true. Indeed, many of the truths and beliefs that we hold, both individually and as a society, are arbitrary and may shock those belonging to other cultures. For example, people in certain Eastern societies believe that cows and mice are more holy than humans. We should regard with suspicion personal beliefs that disempower us—their "truth" is highly likely to be inaccurate.

Beliefs are held in memory in the subconscious mind. Because everything in subconsciousness is below our radar—that is, not in our conscious awareness—beliefs tend to be invisible. They are invisible but not inaccessible. Consequently, the beliefs we have made a point of identifying and remembering, such as key religious beliefs, are known to us. However, most people haven't thought about or identified core beliefs about themselves. It's as if we are born with an "inactive circuit" in this regard. This could be regarded as a design flaw in the way we are wired to operate. I say this because if we understand our personal beliefs, we are in a great position to manage them. Doing so gives us the ability to put our hands right on the steering wheel of our lives.

Well, keep reading, because understanding and knowing how to identify and manage your beliefs is exactly where we are heading.

The Significance of Personal Beliefs

Beliefs about ourselves (which I'll call personal beliefs) and other core beliefs about life, people, and values are enormously important. These are very significant beliefs because they form a multidimensional network or framework that limits and shapes our thoughts, feelings, and behaviour. They shape the reality of life that we experience.

For example, let's take two groups of people who had consistency in what their parents, teachers, and friends said and did as they grew up. The people whose experiences led them to believe they were very special and deeply loved would, by the time they came to their teen years, have a completely different sense of self and of life than those in an identical physical environment whose experiences led them to constantly feel worthless and unloved. Our beliefs are formed in response to our experiences—particularly the experiences that are repeated over time.

All the characteristics of our personalities are shaped by our beliefs. Beliefs determine whether we are selfish, generous, short-tempered, patient, depressed, superficial, gregarious, and so on. Beliefs determine our perceptions. They constrain our imaginations and our thinking. This is encapsulated in that famous quote attributed to Henry Ford: "Whether you think [i.e. believe] you can or you can't, you are right." Thus, if we believe that we don't have an artistic bone in our bodies, our efforts at art will be hopeless until we change that belief or do something to help change it. If someone who believed this took on an art training course for several months, it is very likely that the experiences and the expertise developed during that time would lead them to a new belief—that they now *do* have artistic talent.

The point here is that we are all capable of so much more than we give ourselves credit. Beliefs limit what is possible. However, in essence, beliefs are thoughts, and thoughts can be changed. If we identify limiting beliefs and are willing to change them, we can expand what is possible for ourselves.

Where to Look to Find Beliefs About Yourself

Beliefs manifest themselves in our thoughts, feelings, speech, actions, and behaviour. Turn your attention to these if you want to find your beliefs. Notice those thoughts and feelings that are positive and those that are negative. Then look for the beliefs involved; you will find one or more appropriate beliefs behind each one.

To get us started, let's look in some detail at one important area: fears.

Fears

Fear is very useful in life-and-death situations because it is intensely motivating. When we are fearful, our bodies react, preparing us for fight or flight. Our hearts beat faster, adrenaline pours into our bloodstreams, and our senses and focus are heightened. That's great if our lives depend on getting out of a dangerous situation.

Fears are part of the reality that all people experience, but these days, few are triggered by life-threatening circumstances. Most of our fears are about security and what I will call "looking good." In other words, many fears are a response to perceived threats to the immature, less developed part of our subconscious mind, previously referred to as our junior autopilot. We don't have to focus on this to allow it to influence us because it's right there all the time, at a subconscious level.

Different Manifestations of Fear

Fears manifest in different ways. One way is specific fear, such as the anxiety before a performance or test. Another is nonspecific fear, sometimes called free-floating anxiety. You may have experienced this when you woke up in the night or first thing in the morning feeling worried or anxious but couldn't put your finger on exactly why. Fear also manifests as anger, agitation, and irritability. Yes, anger *is* a manifestation of fear. If you identify and remove the fear, your anger will dissipate. This is why many psychologists say there are only two primary emotions: fear and love.

The Beliefs Behind Our Fears

Behind each fear, there is a belief—a disempowering belief. Let's consider some possible examples:

- Fear: anxiety about money

  Belief: "I'm never going to have enough money."

- Fear: anxiety about time

  Belief: "There's so much to do and so little time. I mustn't waste time!"

- Fear: anxiety about your child

  Belief: "[Child's name] isn't capable of being successful without my help and protection. I must look after him/her."

Why It's Important to Manage Your Fears

It is important to manage fears for several reasons.

- The most important reason is that every fear is a signal that attracts to you exactly what it is that you fear. Their messages travel out through subconsciousness, and by the law of attraction, they attract the circumstances that are consistent with the fear signals: lack of money, the absence of a lover, or an (apparently) incompetent child, for example.

- Fears ruminate in our subconsciousness. Our subconscious mind directs and controls all the automatic functions in our bodies—our growth, the beating of our hearts, the release of hormones, and so on. Our state of mind impacts the subconsciously managed functions of our body, almost certainly including the functioning of the complex immune system. Happiness and laughter have positive effects on the body, while anger, fear, and other negative emotions have a negative impact. Therefore, I recommend that you don't put up with fears—do something about them.

- Perhaps the most obvious reason for managing our fears is so we feel better, happier, and lighter. This frees up our attention, which allows greater creativity. Fears hook our attention and anchor it. Freedom from fear releases it.

How to Manage Your Fears

To manage your fears, you must identify and face them. You must be in action. Once you have identified a fear, you are in a position to manifest its opposite—faith or trust. The best way to implement these is to create a positive, empowering belief to replace the limiting belief.

- Money: "I am a money magnet! I share in the abundance of the universe!"

- Time: "I have plenty of time to do everything I need to do."

- Your child: "[Child's name] is finding his/her own way to success. I support him/her with my love."

If you find that the affirmation doesn't feel right, it won't work. If that's the case, modify it slightly and use the modification until the original does feel right. You can modify the affirmation by adding the phrase, *I am learning to be* or, *I am becoming*, before the affirmation.

Affirmations strengthen your beliefs. However, they won't have any effect if your actions, thoughts, and words are contrary to them. Consistent messages to subconsciousness will produce the changes that you want.

Let's look at managing the fear of public speaking as an example.

- You must understand exactly what it is about public speaking that you fear. This fear may reflect low self-esteem: you value what others think of you more than your own thoughts about yourself. Take the time to identify the exact factor responsible for this fear.

- Next, you must know what you want—for example, to be confident and effective or to enjoy public speaking.

- Knowing this, you can start work on improving your beliefs about yourself: make them become areas of strength. Put your new belief(s) into one or more affirmations. Remember, the affirmations need to ring true to you. For a self-esteem issue, you might select "I am (or, I am becoming ever more) courageous and confident in expressing myself to others." Say your new affirmation(s) frequently.

- Here is another important step: make a list of the evidence that proves that your new belief and affirmation is true, and the reasons why this is so. Keep working on this list every week. Keep saying your affirmation throughout the day and when you go to bed until you know you have achieved transformation in this area.

- Also, be in action. Practise being the confident person you would like to be. Become so well rehearsed in doing this that you can step into the role at will. Believe you can do it; live into that belief. Look for opportunities to speak in public, and keep practising.

What I have just described is the process for resolving deep-seated fears. Are you willing to take action on yours?

A Technique to Reveal Beliefs

Until you have a good degree of experience looking for and finding beliefs, it isn't easy to spot them. The best way is to think as if you are somebody else. Sounds weird? Let's look at this exercise, undertaken by Dayna, from my coaching file.

She emailed the following:

"I'm stuck in my relationship with the people at work, especially with my head of department. It began when a position for which I am qualified came up in my business team and someone more junior was promoted ahead of me. I've talked to the head of the department twice about this, but he hasn't given me a believable answer about why I didn't get the job. Now I feel awkward with the person who got the job and with my boss. I'm unhappy at work. This happened two months ago. I'm feeling intensely frustrated, and now I don't know how much longer I'll be able to stay there."

To help her find the limiting beliefs that were destroying the quality of her life in the job, I asked Dayna this question: "What beliefs might someone have if he or she felt overwhelming frustration at not knowing why someone else was promoted ahead of him or her?" I asked her to brainstorm as many possible beliefs that might answer this question, without any judgement about the answers she came up with. I emphasized that she must not spend time at this stage deciding whether the beliefs were correct or not.

She made the following lists of possible beliefs:

1. *Beliefs about myself*

    - People don't respect my opinions.

    - I'm not good enough.

- People don't trust me.
- There's no point in trying.
- I'm fatally flawed. I'll never be successful.

2. *Beliefs about others involved*

- My boss is deceitful.
- My boss is too old for his job.
- The people here are "up themselves."

With these ideas as a starting point, the next step was for her to go over them and feel for her inner response to each. Which ones felt right or resonated with her? She did this and decided that *I'm not good enough* was the deep-rooted key belief sabotaging her. We decided not to put any attention right now on the beliefs about others.

It is possible to spend time looking back to find where a key limiting belief might have started. Personally, I don't think it really matters that much. The more important task is the one that follows.

Replace Disempowering Beliefs With Ones That Empower You

I'm not good enough is a belief that is never going to help you achieve much. In fact, it is likely to hold you back. I asked Dayna to think up a new belief that would help, not hinder. She would then use this new belief to replace the old one.

To do this, she used the same technique that was used in the previous section. She thought as if she were someone else and asked herself, "What beliefs might a confident, successful person have in my situation?" Then she brainstormed to find answers. The new beliefs she created were "I am inspired and unstoppable in every part of my life" and "I am conscientious and respected; I go the extra mile."

Again, I asked her to feel for the belief that really felt right. She chose the first one, but with a slight modification: "I am unstoppable!" With this belief in place, she looked again at her job and the issues she had been facing. Without any further advice from me, she got into action.

Standing in the belief "I am unstoppable," she asked her boss for an anonymous performance review from him and her work colleagues. She later explained to me that her purpose was to find out what she could be doing better and whether there was an area in which she needed extra training. Her boss agreed, and the feedback was very helpful. Yes, they all thought Dayna was conscientious and reliable, but they thought that she needed to do more to be an effective part of the team. Several people said that she often kept ideas to herself and that she needed to be more open and share ideas well before it was nearly time for final decisions to be made.

Dayna wrote to me, "What a great outcome! As a result of looking at my beliefs and replacing the one that was limiting me, new possibilities immediately appeared. I got over my anger and frustration, and work has never been more stimulating. Everyone on the team seems happier; they are a great bunch!"

Creating empowering beliefs is definitely the most important step in managing your beliefs. It is not critical to find the disempowering beliefs; it *is* critical to create and use empowering ones.

Having said this, discovering your old limiting beliefs is valuable (1) because it is a self-learning process and (2) because it enables you to identify these beliefs again when they resurface. Once you have made them visible, it is much easier to spot them at work again.

Managing Your Beliefs: Keep a List

Longstanding, deeply-rooted beliefs are not going to change in the first week after you decide to replace them. They may have been around for decades. Even when you think they are gone, they can re-emerge and reassert themselves.

I recommend that you keep a list of the beliefs you create for yourself. My own list includes beliefs about

- my body—that it is an automatically self-healing system that always operates perfectly; that my immune system functions perfectly and harmoniously with the other parts of my body;

- my mind;

- finances;

- the people in my life; and

- what I stand for in relation to humanity.

By itself, creating your list will have little effect. However, if you read the list every day, you can memorize it. Practise saying it to yourself every day—perhaps when you get up, before you go to bed, or on your way to work.

Summary

1. Beliefs are important thoughts that are held in memory in the subconscious mind. They are important because they are "the truth" for us.

2. Beliefs remain outside our awareness until we go looking for them.

3. Beliefs are developed as a result of experience. The experiences may be major single events, but many beliefs arrive and take root because of what our parents (especially) and others have said or done repeatedly to us.

4. Beliefs manifest themselves in our thoughts, feelings, speech, actions, and behaviour. They directly influence our perception of what happens in our lives. More than that, because they are the fundamental determinant of our thoughts and feelings and because these in turn activate the law of attraction, ultimately, it is our beliefs that are the cause of the circumstances, experiences, and quality of life we experience, as well as the reason why we attract the people we attract.

5. When we look for and find the beliefs—positive and negative—that are running our lives and then actively manage them, we begin the process of taking charge of our lives. However, it's like going to school, learning to play a new instrument, or using new complicated software: it's not easy at first, but it gets easier as we persist. Mistakes are part of the learning process.

6. Keep a written record of the beliefs that support you, and use it frequently.

Practice

1. Create a list of things you fear. Look for them in your thoughts, feelings, speech, actions, and behaviour.

    - Listen while you are talking to others and notice when you spot a fear in there; listen especially carefully when you are complaining, criticizing, or blaming.

- Notice when you feel angry, anxious, stressed, upset, or depressed; you will be able to locate a fear there too.

2. Look for the limiting belief behind each fear. A method for doing this is described above in the section "A Technique to Reveal Beliefs."

3. Create an empowering belief to replace the one that has been limiting you. Be sure to write down all the new beliefs you create and read them at least once every day. Enjoy the feeling of recreating your life in this way. This is *not* a chore!

4. Are there any memories that cause anxiety or upset? Perhaps you have memories of upsetting experiences in your childhood, in an earlier job, or with a former friend, acquaintance, or lover.

5. Find the negative beliefs that are causing or contributing to the feeling of upset—perhaps by identifying what you wanted, as opposed to what actually happened—and create new beliefs that will, with practice, dissolve these past upsets. This is great work. You are now creating inner freedom.

6. Set your mental radar so that it alerts you whenever an old fear (and its limiting beliefs) resurfaces. When this happens, you can immediately say your chosen belief to yourself and get back on track.

CHAPTER 9
CREATING MOMENTUM

> Procrastination makes easy things
> hard, hard things harder.
> —Mason Cooley

We have spent time in this book looking at the way we create our lives. If you have gotten this far into the book, you are someone who is interested in making progress. You want to get rid of outworn habits and do things better. This chapter deals with one of the most important habits that cramps creativity, slows momentum, and causes recurrent annoyance and frustration. I'm talking about procrastination.

Procrastination has been defined in various ways. In a nutshell, it refers to putting off doing a necessary task in order to avoid something. It is the result of mental resistance to being in action. Our aim—mine and yours—is to be intentional and purposeful in creating now. Procrastination is neither of these. It is definitely a hindrance to achieving what we want.

The Cause of Procrastination: Some Kind of Benefit

Different factors may trigger us to avoid taking action. We may procrastinate completing tax returns, for instance, because it will require effort in areas where there is no direct benefit to ourselves. We may want to avoid boredom or avoid missing out on a more pleasurable activity, so we procrastinate, putting off the task before us.

Not knowing exactly how to do something or not knowing exactly what we want can also trigger procrastination. Fear is another common motivator. Here, the benefit is not having to face or experience what we fear. Psychologists have identified poor self-esteem as an important factor in people who have strongly procrastinating behaviours: they avoid things that may threaten their self-worth.

Very often, procrastination is motivated by a desire to stay within one's comfort zone. Well, guess what? The comfort zone is the topic of the next chapter.

The Cost

Inherent in the term *procrastination* is the potential for consequences that are triggered by putting off the necessary task. A late tax return may well result in a penalty. When we don't say something important to another person—whether it is to ask him or her out on a date or confront him or her on an issue where he or she is out of line—there are consequences. Life takes another direction in each of these last two examples because we have passed up on an opportunity that could have made a difference in our lives and in that of the other person. Sure, it may be a little confrontational to ask someone out on a first date or to take issue with another person, but in both cases, by not taking those actions, you've lost out on potentially great friendships and character growth from being courageous.

Because procrastination is an avoidance technique, it sends a strong message to our subconsciousness that we *need* to avoid certain things. There are things we cannot cope with. There are fears we cannot handle. This is perhaps the worst part of the procrastination habit—it is self-fulfilling and self-sustaining. Worse, it is self-destructive.

The Way Out of Procrastination

We procrastinate when we are on autopilot. Procrastination is a failure to take direct responsibility for managing something. The first step to freedom is to acknowledge that the price for procrastination is too high. You can make the choice now to end the procrastination habit. Being intentional about this and looking for opportunities to be active sends an important message to the subconscious mind, letting it know that you will no longer put up with procrastination.

Making the decision to eliminate procrastination forever is very powerful and positive. The benefits are immense. You will have less anxiety, less stress, and greater satisfaction from having things under control. You are eliminating the nasty surprises and unpleasant consequences that result from putting things off.

The second step to breaking yourself of this habit is to become aware of the particular things you put off till later. Find the things you have procrastinated doing until now. We are going to call these things your *potential procrastination items* or PPIs. Make a list so you have them clearly identified and earmarked so that you can make a special effort to manage them effectively from now on.

The third step is to make sure you have a way of organizing what you do so procrastination doesn't happen. Let's look briefly at that now. We will look at the details later, in chapter 13, "Systems That Work," and chapter 15, "Target What You Most Want."

Keep Track of What You Are Managing

It's very easy to get into the habit of just focusing on the main thing in life that we are interested in. Studying for a degree, setting out on a busy new career, or having a baby are just a few examples of situations in which people find themselves totally engrossed in one aspect of their lives, almost to the exclusion of everything else. This is quite normal, but it isn't inevitable. You can do better.

The way to do better is to be well organized beforehand or make the time and effort to get organized on the job. Here are a few ways to keep organized:

- Keep a list of all the things that you are managing. Include every corner of your life.

  You might use a whiteboard, your computer, or sheets of paper in a folder.

- With each project or goal, list the various steps or different areas that will need attention. Then add as many tasks as you can identify for each step.

- Identify small stuff as well as the big stuff. Give priority to things like communicating with family and friends and planning travel well ahead of time. Being proactive means there's much less chance of missing out.

- Keep your task list up to date; make changes every week, at least, or more often when appropriate.

- Use Microsoft Outlook or another calendar system to show future activities. Keep that up to date too.

Make Being Organized and Ending Procrastination a Game

Don't make any part of your life unnecessarily hard. Make it fun by using your imagination. Make sure you know your previous and current potential procrastination items. Give them special attention and priority.

You don't have to manage life alone. Why not enrol a friend in the process of ending procrastination and getting organized? Give each other a list of your PPIs and keep score of your successes. Keep a success diary. Challenge each other. Transform the procrastination weakness into strength.

Love how it feels to be properly organized. Become known as the person who gets things done.

Summary

1. Procrastination is a destructive, *very* costly habit. Don't put up with it. Don't let it run any part of your life.

2. Start a list of the things that you procrastinate over—your PPIs. Keep adding to the list as you identify them.

3. Get organized. This is the way out of being a procrastinator. Start a weekly task list. This can be done on paper, or you can find an app to use on your phone, e-pad, or computer. Decide which will work best for you. Put reminders into your e-calendar about important tasks or events.

4. Make sure that your must-do tasks (which will include your PPIs) are highlighted. Do not give yourself permission to not do any of them.

5. Make a total commitment to use your weekly task list every single day.

    - Make sure you keep the practice up—no misses whatsoever—for at least six weeks. By then, the habit will be 90 per cent reliable.

    - If you have a holiday, keep using the task list. The items will be very different on holiday, but there's no need to stop. By stopping, you will interrupt this important habit.

6. Schedule the time to plan your life. Set the time aside every week. Show up enthusiastically at these appointment times. Plan today, tomorrow, the week, the month, and the year: make life happen!

7. No more poor planning! No more procrastination! Make getting organized and putting an end to procrastination an enjoyable project. Enjoy this aspect of creating now.

Practice

1. Make a list now of some of the things you have procrastinated doing up till now. Pick one and ask yourself the following questions:

    - What were the benefits of putting it off?

    - What were the costs?

2. Make the decision to put an end to tolerating procrastination in your life. Record the date on which you commit to this decision.

3. Make a list of things you procrastinate doing.

4. If putting an end to procrastination doesn't feel like a fairly easy thing to do, pick a friend or a colleague to be a buddy with whom you take it on. Make sure, though, that there is no way you will wimp out, even if that person does. Taking on a buddy provides a support structure to guarantee success, as long as there is zero risk that you will be drawn into the other person's failure, should that occur.

5. Organize yourself.

    - Create a visual display of what you are managing: include every area of your life.

    - Create and use a weekly task list. (This is discussed in detail in chapter 13.)

6. Set rules for yourself. Commit to

    - scheduling the time each week and each month to review and plan your activities;

    - scheduling a time each day—early in the day—when you will start working with your weekly task list; and

    - making enjoyment, happiness, and achievement happen in many areas of your life every single day.

CHAPTER 10

BEYOND YOUR COMFORT ZONE, BEYOND THE FAMILIAR

We all know what a comfort zone is because we have heard about it and realize that to some extent we live there at least some of the time. Living within one's comfort zone is a great example of operating on autopilot—that is, with subconsciousness in charge. If our conscious minds were fully engaged, we would be constantly examining the various aspects of our lives and actively managing them. We would be constantly aware of what we want and would be going for it.

Characteristics of the Comfort Zone

Familiarity and stability are key elements of the comfort zone. Actually, *comfort zone* is not an accurate term. The correct one is *familiarity zone*. *Comfort* implies the ability to relax, and living in one's comfort zone may not be relaxing; examples of this are living with an alcoholic or someone who physically or mentally beats you up. However, *comfort zone* is a term that is widely used and is well understood. But wait a minute—it's familiar, and despite its deficiency, we put up with it. So using this very term *comfort zone* is an example of living within our comfort zones.

Another characteristic of the comfort zone is predictability, because we know what's likely to happen or we know how to respond. Therefore, less effort is required. We don't have to think! We don't have to be creative. We can relax because we know. Unfortunately, this characteristic is not conducive to improvement, let alone excellence. It fosters mediocrity, sloppy thinking, sloppy habits, and sloppy behaviour. If you want to be admired, want to get ahead, or just want satisfaction from life, the comfort zone is not the place to be.

Living Within Our Comfort Zone May Not Be Easy

There may be aspects of living in our comfort zones that make us unhappy. Lack of satisfaction or actual pain can become so familiar that we learn to put up with it automatically. Perhaps because we are able to tolerate the level of pain or because changing the situation seems too hard, we have, consciously or unconsciously, decided not to strive for something better. We'll look at what you can do in this type of situation shortly.

Is It Bad to Live Inside the Comfort Zone?

Living in your comfort zone isn't necessarily a bad thing. It's the percentage of your life in which you operate there, and the degree to which you restrict or limit your opportunities and the use of your mind that determine whether or not being in your comfort zone may be negatively impacting your life or the people around you. Being in your comfort zone can be positive if it truly enables happiness, providing a nurturing, stimulating environment in which you are living a creative, productive life. Just how much productivity is enough is your business, not mine.

The Pros and Cons

Most of the time, living within the comfort zone is robbing us of life. As with procrastination, there is always a payoff and a cost to living within the comfort zone.

- The payoff is that the comfort zone protects us from the unknown. It protects us from being challenged.
- The cost is that the comfort zone inhibits learning new skills. It inhibits creativity and limits interest, excitement, and growth.

Potential Signs of Living Inside Your Comfort Zone

- procrastinating
- being emotionally dependent on another person (You "need" that person for a particular purpose—so you feel happy, don't feel lonely, or feel more complete)
- frequently being bored for weeks, months, or years
- watching hours of TV most days
- texting or playing video games for hours most days
- being addicted to work, relaxing activities (i.e. not work), food, smoking, alcohol, or shopping
- wearing the same old clothes month after month, year after year
- eating the same food again and again

- avoiding meeting new people

- avoiding speaking up when it's important to say something

- avoiding anything that looks like a challenge

- putting up with dysfunctional people or situations that are upsetting

- putting up with being overweight, unfit, or tired

- putting up with feeling depressed, unhappy, or used

- not contributing to the people around you

- "using" people

- blaming others for your situation or your problems

You may have found items on this list that apply to you. However, you can easily rationalize them—they *are* appropriate. But I say, "Excuses, excuses." No matter what excellent reason you have, the reality is that you have been operating inside your comfort zone—period.

Do You Need to Change Anything?

This is the wrong question to ask. The list of potential signs in the previous section was designed to help you identify where in life you are or have been on autopilot, in order to open up the potential for having more possibilities—more opportunities for excitement, for satisfaction, and most importantly, for getting more of what you want.

Do not focus on what you *need* to change; find out what you *want* to change. That is your starting point. Having read the list of signs, there may be things you want to change right now. Perhaps you can see that it's appropriate to apologize to someone, to unlock your heart and give your love freely, to stop doing some things and start doing others. But before you do, take a little time to clearly identify what it is that you want—what your goal is—in making these changes. Add that to your list of goals, if you have one; if you don't, start a list of goals and include this one.

If there is no immediate action you feel you want to take, start the process of looking at what you want and go from there.

**Make a Habit of Challenging Yourself—
Explore the Richness of Life**

It's a healthy practice to frequently step out beyond the comfort zone of the familiar. Challenge yourself to do a little more, a little better. It's stimulating to do so. It wakes us up and allows new ideas and opportunities to arise. Make a habit of looking at what you can do differently just for the sake of exploring the richness of experience. Changes don't have to be monumental. Start with simple things. Here are some ideas; you will find more in chapter 7, "Engage Your Imagination":

- Take a different route than usual.

- Have something different to eat—something healthy.

- Go without alcohol.

- Improve your behaviour (e.g., give compliments, thank people sincerely as you look them in the eye).

- Improve your outlook (e.g., be confident, optimistic, and focused on success).

- Identify things you have been tolerating and deal with them (e.g., get rid of messes).

Some new things will bring unexpected pleasure, others won't. Don't let a negative result or a negative experience put you off.

Don't Charge Into Making Changes

The advice in this heading may or may not be appropriate for you, but in general, it's more important to take ground gradually, gaining more confidence and enjoying the journey as you go. Living inside your comfort zone has served you for a very long time, in all probability. It's a deeply entrenched habit. You can break a habit immediately, but more often than not, the initial rush of energy then starts to wane. Before you know it, you are back where you started or maybe worse off because you "failed."

The reason why charging into implementing change doesn't often result in a lasting new habit is that being in the comfort zone is an automatic activity, a habit that is rooted in the subconscious mind. It has been pointed out earlier that one of the properties of the subconscious mind is homeostasis—keeping things the same. This doesn't mean you can't change things. In order to create now most effectively, we want the conscious mind to be the master and the subconscious mind to be the servant. But servants only do their jobs well if you treat them correctly. You don't demand or force servants if you want to keep them. You treat them with respect, the way you want to be treated. A little subtlety goes a long way towards success in installing new habits.

My suggestion is to start with first things first. Choose one thing that is manageable—not necessarily the one thing you most want to change. Implement the change very slowly. If you want to spend more time reading instead of watching TV, start the first week by switching off the TV half an hour earlier to do your reading. The next week, switch off the TV an hour earlier. Gradually increase the time over the next few weeks. It may be six weeks before you don't switch on the TV at all some nights of the week.

Developing the will-power "muscle" takes time, just as getting fit at a gym or swimming pool takes persistence over time.

When the Comfort Zone Is Painful

Some people feel like they don't have a choice: they are unhappy in their situations, but they can't see a way out. They are trapped. They are victims to the circumstances. That is their belief. Now, just to be clear, I am a coach, not a counsellor. However, being a victim is a horrible thing. I don't recommend that anyone put up with this type of situation. Get advice. This may well involve seeing a counsellor. Reading books about the subject may also help get you started.

Here are some more suggestions to get you moving in the right direction:

- Identify what you want—that's the first step. Sometimes people feel so trapped that they have been unable to even do this.

- Know that you deserve better. Your inner beauty is allowed to shine. You are absolutely entitled to be happy and to strive for happiness. Believe in yourself.

- Discover negative beliefs about yourself and about others involved in your situation, and replace those beliefs with positive ones. For example:

    - "I deserve an abundance of life's riches."

- "He/she [the other person] is simply doing the best he/ she can."

Chapter 8 deals with beliefs and fears. It would be best to work with the materials there if you are in a painful comfort zone and are serious about extricating yourself from it.

- Be compassionate and forgiving with yourself and with the others involved.

- Ask for help. Look for help, as explained in the previous paragraph.

- Focus on your strengths. If you see weaknesses, work on them and turn them into strengths.

- Change yourself; do not try to change other people. They are responsible for themselves. You have no responsibility and no right to try and change others. Trying to change another (particularly in painful circumstances) is doomed to failure.

- Later, it will be obvious to you that these painful circumstances are a gift that is giving you the opportunity to grow into a more effective, creative, and wonderful person!

Transitioning from Comfortable to Extraordinary

The main purpose of this chapter has been to explain the comfort zone, with its costs and benefits, and to show that it involves living mainly on autopilot. I have shown how to make adjustments and where to look so that you can decide where to start adjusting in order to move or move faster out of your comfort zone, if that's what you decide is right for you.

However, that is just the start. The real "juice" in life is arriving at the extraordinary—in terms of happiness, success, creativity, excitement, connection with people, enjoyment, contribution, and achievement—in whatever aspect of aspiration and endeavour you choose. You probably know the first step towards this high-performance state. It is the same one you make when making any change: know what you want. Develop a crystal clear vision of this. Next, generate and keep generating an intense desire for this extraordinary goal. That desire is your ticket. It is the engine room of power and motivation that will take you to the journey's end.

Then, on the journey to attaining your goal, strive to challenge yourself: do what it takes, knowing that nothing can prevent your success. Be prepared to learn skills that you currently have no idea you will need. Organize yourself and take full responsibility for manifesting your dream or vision in physical form. I'll talk more about this soon.

Maybe you are not ready to challenge yourself in the way I have just suggested. That's okay. You can choose when the time is right, and in the meantime be challenging yourself in gradually increasing ways as suggested earlier in this chapter. However, if you are someone who is already lined up on the runway, ready to take off into high performance and excellence, really use the information I've given you in this chapter and in the rest of this book. I know you will make that transition, and I'm so excited for you!

Summary

1. The comfort zone isn't really a happy place. It's boring. Sometimes it's painful.

2. Stepping out of the comfort zone into the challenge zone is a healthy habit to develop. That's the place where giving the most to life and getting the most from it begins.

3. Taking charge of life isn't difficult; it just requires a system of managing things—a system that involves writing things down, *not* attempting to keep them in your mind.

4. Henry Ford said, "There isn't a man or woman alive who can't do more than they think they can." I agree. Expanding the limits of what's possible in your (and my) life involves creating challenges and stepping outside the zone of comfort.

5. Leaving your comfort zone doesn't have to be hard. Make it interesting. Make it fun.

6. Start with baby steps. Start small, going for what you want. Start now. Gradually pick up the pace as you gain experience.

7. The ultimate challenge is aiming high at something extraordinary, making the comfort zone a thing of the past.

Practice

1. Go back and look at the list of signs of living in the comfort zone. Ask yourself if any of them apply to you. Most likely, some will.

2. Make it a practice to challenge yourself every day. Make a list of challenges, and then do one every day. Also, look for opportunities to spontaneously challenge yourself to do better.

3. Make a list of what you want. What are the things you want to change?

4. Select the thing you are going to work on first. Start with something that you know you can achieve.

5. Make a plan in which you schedule, gradually introduce, and increase the amount of time you spend doing the new activity.

6. If you find the plan is too tough, ease up a little—adjust the plan. There is no urgency, and you can't force your way to success. If you are forcing, you are almost certainly heading towards failure.

7. If your self-discipline should lapse, don't judge yourself; just get back on track. Identify why the lapse occurred, and do what it takes to make sure it doesn't happen again.

8. Learn from your mistakes; don't beat yourself (or anyone else) up for making a mistake.

9. Build on your success. When you have eliminated one comfort-zone behaviour, move on to the next one. Again, be subtle as you start working on it.

10. Keep adjusting your goals. Maybe you are ready to aim high right now. Eventually almost everyone will want to aim for extraordinary—things like high performance, abundance, generosity, and excellent service. You will have your personal vision of how this looks. Why not schedule the time right now to start working on it soon?

CHAPTER 11

EFFECTIVE COMMUNICATION

> The single biggest problem in communication
> is the illusion that it has taken place.
> —George Bernard Shaw

Creating the lives we want and love to lead is an ongoing process. We have been looking at a number of things we want to manage purposefully. Communicating effectively with other people is another important area to pay attention to. Communication between human beings is more difficult than we may realize. Have you noticed when speaking to someone that you said exactly what you meant but they interpreted it as meaning something quite different? Or that they said something and you either misunderstood or had no idea what they were getting at?

Why is communication so difficult? As this chapter progresses, you will discover the answers to this question. Keep in mind that communication is always a two-way process and that it involves speaking and listening. However, as we are about to find out, there are more than two things to manage at the same time.

Listening

Listening as a Speaker

No, the heading "Listening as a Speaker" doesn't mean that I have lapsed into gibberish. The point I'm making in this heading is that even when we are speaking to another person, we need to listen to ourselves. You've heard people who don't do this, usually when they are excited. They babble away at 100 km/hr—exceeding the speed limit for safe (i.e. effective) talking and listening. What comes out is most often unconsidered rubbish.

So the first rules as a speaker are to think before you speak and to listen while you do. We don't always get it right, but listening to ourselves as we speak reduces the chance for mistakes and enables us to quickly make adjustments if an error occurs.

Listening as a Listener

The biggest mistake we make when listening is to listen as the speaker starts, but then switch to listening to *yourself* as you decide what you are going to say in reply.

When someone is speaking, give the speaker all of your attention or none of your attention. If the speaker is mouthing off at you, don't buy into it. Stay in your own mental space, and decide if the matter needs to be reframed into a non-dysfunctional context or if it is irrelevant to you.

If you are going to listen, listen with 100 per cent of your attention. There is no need to get hooked by what's being said; just "get" the communication. That's all you need to do as a listener.

Listen for What's Unspoken

Besides listening to what is said, also "listen" for the unspoken communication—for what is not said.

- Listen for the other person's passion or excitement.

- Listen for the other person's pain.

- Listen for what's important to the other person.

- Listen to what it's like from that person's perspective, standing in his or her shoes.

When we listen for all this, we are listening with empathy, compassion, and caring. We are listening without judgement. Our ability to contribute usefully goes up enormously when we engage these extra powers of listening.

If you are in any service situation, this way of listening will improve your service—it will make what you contribute invaluable. People will remember you for the right reasons.

Listening to Yourself: Mind Chatter

It's very difficult to stop having thoughts. The mind keeps up an almost constant flow of chatter that results in human beings having tens of thousands of thoughts every day. Not everything the mind thinks is beneficial—in fact, it can be the exact opposite. We tend to make judgements all the time about everything that comes to our attention.

- "Oh, there's another Nissan. They're ugly."

- "Wow, he is gorgeous."

- "I wish they'd fix those traffic lights. I hate waiting!"

- "That person is a dropout if ever I saw one."

We are critical of others, but most people are also very critical of themselves. Have you ever done something dumb and thought to yourself, *You idiot!* You have probably thought even worse things about yourself.

When we allow these self-critical thoughts to go unchecked, they are destructive. They do not empower us. Quite the opposite—we disempower ourselves.

Internal mind chatter comes from the subconscious mind. Judgements and negative thoughts there have been with us for a very long time, probably since our early years of life. Most likely, we learned the disempowering thoughts and the names we suddenly shout at ourselves back in our early years. We may have become used to hearing them and don't even think about them when they arise. We may just suddenly feel sad, unloved, or angry with ourselves without knowing exactly how or why.

Retraining Your Inner Commentator

It's important to not ignore your inner commentator. If the messages it gives you are not to your liking, make up your mind to retrain it!

If you hear your inner commentator/mind chatter abusing or criticizing you, here's what to do:

1. Make yourself aware of what has happened; identify the negative or self-destructive thought.

2. Nurture yourself. Comfort the vulnerable, innocent you that just took this hit of abuse. Take your time over this stage.

> This has been going on for too long, and that vulnerable part of you has an enormous amount of healing to do.

3. Create a positive thought about yourself; perhaps say to yourself a positive affirmation you have previously prepared.

Notice particularly step two: the advice is not to recognize the negative thought and to displace it immediately with a positive one. Even if we already have a habit of deleting these negative thoughts rapidly from our consciousness, that does not alter the habit. The harmful thoughts just keep on coming.

When we spend time on step two, the nurturing intention sends a definite message to subconsciousness: "I'm not tolerating these kinds of harmful thoughts about myself any more. I care for myself. I don't hate myself anymore." Truly, this is a major step towards expanding your love nature.

Meditation

We will look at meditation in more detail in chapter 16. However, we need to start on it now, because meditation is a way—a really valuable way—of becoming aware of and gradually reducing mind chatter. One important part of meditation is emptying the mind of everything except the subject or object on which you are meditating. This might be a physical object, a guided journey, or a topic such as having compassion, having gratitude, being part of the All, or resolving a particular problem. Unless you are already practised in meditation, self-directed meditation is particularly likely to result in thoughts, or mind chatter.

When meditating, the conscious mind is active in a focused way. You start by placing your attention on the subject of the meditation, but you also expand your awareness to your breath, your body, and the sounds around you. The meditation subject or object should evoke a positive feeling, an emotion, an energy. Holding that energy, relax (but don't completely let go of) your awareness of your breath, of your body, and of sounds. Your mind is now in a state of heightened awareness and heightened presence—it is open to life.

Sooner or later thoughts arrive. If they are unhelpful and distracting and grab (anchor) your attention, your conscious mind has the task of deciding that this is just automatic thinking, or mind chatter, and bringing your awareness back to the meditation object, your breath, your body, and the sounds. Thoughts are thus quietly and peacefully ignored. Often mind chatter is easy to identify because it has nothing to do with the subject of the meditation.

After meditating, it is helpful to spend a couple of minutes recalling when mind chatter was going on so that you get more and more skilled in identifying it. You are then in a much better position to refocus. These skills will transfer into the non-meditative parts of your life, increasing your awareness and ability to focus.

Think about that last sentence. Read it again. There is a gem in that last sentence that you can build on. It takes practice to empty your mind of thoughts and to politely show them the door when they try to get in. Once you can do this, an additional, invaluable practice is to do a few thirty- to sixty-second mini-meditations every day: empty your mind of everything except your intention, which is your commitment to centre yourself. Then put your awareness on your breath, your body, and the sounds around you. Do this for thirty to sixty seconds. That's all.

This is an incredibly powerful practice in which you are providing ongoing training for the conscious and the subconscious parts of your mind. Please, do it for yourself and for the people you love. Before long they will be commenting on the difference in you, and you too will be aware of the change that has happened from this one practice.

Speaking

Non-verbal Communication: Knowing When to Speak

You know, it isn't always necessary to speak to communicate. We can do so with a look, with our posture, and even with our presence or absence. Sometimes, it is more powerful to say nothing. There are times when it is better to keep our own counsel rather than declaring our interest or opening up an aspect of ourselves to someone whose opinion we don't respect. Knowing when to speak and when to keep silent is a great skill that only experience can teach.

The Rules of Language

These days, many consider it cool or trendy to ignore the rules of correct speech. Texting and communicating rapidly by email or other social media have led many to ignore correct spelling and the rules of English and other languages. Does this matter? Language rules were developed to minimize the risk of miscommunication, not to frustrate us. Many people think it probably doesn't matter greatly when they misuse our language. However, errors tend to compound as they are passed on to others—to the next generation for instance. Errors are very likely to confuse people whose first language is not English.

In circumstances where sophisticated, important communication is required—in medicine, politics, finance, law, and vast numbers of other situations—accuracy of language is essential. The more we all make an effort to respect, preserve, and use language accurately, the greater our ability—and that of our community—will become to communicate simply and effectively.

Engaging the Conscious Mind When Speaking

When we speak, it is important to be aware—or in other words, to be present. (Being present is discussed in chapter 3.) However, because much of what we say comes from the subconscious mind, it is easy to be on autopilot when we speak. We can always spot when people who are speaking are not present. Their attention is not on the matter about which are talking. They may be worrying about what others are thinking of them, working out how they can finish on time, or focusing on some other matter instead of giving their attention to what they are saying.

The people who communicate most effectively are in a sort of dance with the people with whom they are communicating. They lead when it is time to lead, pause to create an opportunity for others to speak at appropriate points, and change the direction of the conversation before it gets stuck. To do all this, the conscious mind needs to be alert, aware, and in charge.

We let ourselves down and lose the attention of others and the opportunity to contribute to others both when we withhold and when we rattle on aimlessly. Our communications serve every one best when they are appropriate, interesting, imaginative, and in good humour.

Unhelpful Speech Habits

In the previous section, I mentioned being present (or not) to what we are saying. A classic example of not being present is when people use words and phrases that add nothing positive, while at the same time potentially adding something negative. The phrases *to be honest, what happened was,* and *if you know what I mean* are good examples. Saying *to be honest* adds the clear implication that there are times when you are not honest. Repeatedly saying *if you know what I mean* carries the implication that the speaker thinks the listener is too dumb to know what they mean.

Another speech habit that is less than helpful is to keep punctuating what you are saying with "Okay?" This can be interpreted as an aggressive, even dominating, speech mannerism, as it may be implying, "You had better agree with me, or else." Alternatively, it can be insulting, as it can also be interpreted as an indication that the speaker thinks the listener is too dumb to understand.

I recommend listening carefully when you are speaking. Make sure you eliminate any speech habits that are not serving you.

Say What You Mean and Mean What You Say

Everyone knows that when we say, "I'll think about it," the opposite is invariably true, because we then push the matter to the back of our minds. We often do this when we don't have the information we need to decide what we want. Well why not say so? Practise saying what you really mean rather than slipping into automatic speech to hide the truth.

Words

"I can't." Do you say this? Do you mean that you can't, now or ever, or that you don't want to?

This is a phrase that I suggest you avoid or at least use with care. It sends a message to the subconscious that may well create a barrier to success. This is particularly true if someone is coaching you. In this context, it would be better to say, "I am doing my best at the moment. I will definitely be able to do it with some more practice."

This next point is in the form of a request. Please don't use bad language, swear words, or especially blasphemy. They are ugly, and they too are the product of being unconscious—being asleep to their real meaning. Swear words and blasphemy are unworthy of people who aspire to improve themselves and to contribute to others. They are unworthy of the magnificence of human intellect and creativity.

Choose words that are simple, concise, and effective without the need for over-dramatization. Use words that convey love, beauty, joy, happiness, and aspiration, for these are so much more engaging than their opposites. Our words and language represent us; they herald who we are.

Music in Speech

Music is a powerful mover of our emotions. It may surprise you when I say that there is music in speech, and that this is just as important as, and sometimes more important than the content of what we are saying.

Who do you know anyone who speaks in a monotone? How do you feel when you anticipate talking to them? Who do you find really interesting, and enjoy talking to? Think about the volume, the pitch, the melody, the pace and rhythm of their speech when you are listening to them.

Now, what about you? Do you bring enough emotion or too much emotion into your voice? How does your emotion sound? Does your voice become high-pitched, piercing or squeaky? Do you lose your breath and sound gaspy when you are anxious? What are your speech habits?

There is so much musical information in our speech. The musical aspects of the way we speak conveys a great deal about us to our listeners. Being a great speaker is both an art and a science. Is there potential to improve your voice and the melodies you create with your speech?

If you are interested in learning more about this subject, or increasing the quality and power of your voice for speaking and singing, or improving habits you may not even know you have when speaking publically, I recommend the book, *Set Your Voice Free*, by Roger Love[1].

Summary

1. The difference between being an untrained listener and a skilled listener is immense. It is determined by where we place our attention.

2. Listen to what you are saying, and make sure it is appropriate and clear.

3. When someone else is speaking, don't be passive; choose whether to give all your attention or none to what is being said. Choose whether to engage or not. In this way, you avoid slipping into an automatic, emotional reaction. Instead, you are free to choose to direct the conversation into a more productive direction when this is appropriate.

4. To be successful communicators, we must speak into others' listening. To discover where their listening is focused, we must first discover their concerns, their pain, and their passions. In other words, make a habit of listening for what's important to the people with whom you come into contact.

5. You can train your listening skills by talking about a particular part of your life and examining your listening as you do. Afterwards, write down what you notice. In a short time, you can improve your performance.

6. Being a great listener enables you to connect deeply with people, to empathize with them, and to really appreciate not just them but also yourself.

7. Be aware of and manage your mind chatter. (There's more to do here than just shutting it down.)

8. Choose when to speak and when to hold your counsel. Unnecessary and unworthy words leak and diminish the powers of your mind.

9. Take a stand for improving the standards of the spoken language. Not only does this enable accuracy and prevent misunderstandings, but it also impresses your own consciousness with the powerful and positive intention to demand high standards of yourself.

10. When speaking, stay alert and aware of the circumstances and the listening of others. Do not let your focus drift off into the less important areas that appeal to the subconscious mind.

11. Use words that are uplifting; do not give yourself permission to slip into "gutter speech."

12. What you say is as important as what you do in terms of your effect on others, the messages you are sending to your subconscious mind, and the things you are attracting to yourself.

13. Become more aware of the musical aspects of your own speech. Make the quality of your voice and the melodies you create enjoyable.

Practice

1. Think about how you listen; make a list of the areas or situations in your life in which you can improve your listening.

2. How good are you at communicating?

- How careful are you in articulating what you say with accuracy? Rate yourself. Give yourself a score from zero (worst possible communication) to ten (best possible communication).

- Challenge yourself to be a better, more accurate communicator. Next time you finish a conversation with someone, (silently) give them a score for accurate, straightforward communication, and score yourself. Be honest, and repeat this exercise every day for a week. At the end of the week, see whether your skill as a communicator has changed. What's happened after doing this for a month?

3. Could you benefit from learning new words and adding them to your vocabulary?

    - Reading books and articles can help here, particularly if you jot down and look up the meanings of those words you don't fully understand. This is a great habit; it will expand your knowledge enormously over a period of years.

    - I've heard it suggested that people should go through one page of the dictionary every day, reading everything and making a note of words and their meaning that were either not known or not understood.

4. How often do people ask you to repeat something or say they didn't understand what you said?

- This is not uncommon when you are speaking in a language which is not your native language. If you are in this situation, ask your colleagues, clients, and so on, whether your use of their language is good enough. Are any improvements needed, small or large?

- Consider making it a project to greatly improve your communication abilities. Take lessons to improve your pronunciation and choice of words.

  Your colleagues and clients—even the ones you didn't ask—will show their appreciation. You will get better results, and you will be rewarded for your efforts.

5. If you know your speech needs improvement, consider asking people you trust to point out when you use incorrect grammar, the wrong word, or swear words. We get so familiar with our own speech that a little help with this could be invaluable.

Reference

[1] Roger Love with Donna Frazier. *Set Your Voice Free*. (New York. Little, Brown and Company, 1999)

CHAPTER 12
SIDESTEPPING SUFFERING

> There is a light in this world, a healing spirit more powerful than any darkness we may encounter. We sometimes lose sight of this force when there is suffering, too much pain. Then suddenly, the spirit will emerge through the lives of ordinary people who hear a call and answer in extraordinary ways.
> —Mother Teresa

Suffering in one form or another is a common experience. We are going to approach this topic from several directions in this chapter and from a different one later in this book.

The very word *suffering* conjures up feelings of something very unpleasant, something we want to avoid. The word *suffering* activates one of our primal reflexes—the survival instinct, which is deeply embedded in the subconscious mind. It's not at all surprising, then, that this word does not make us feel happy or empowered.

However, we know that the habit mind can be trained. Before we look at how to use the conscious mind to sidestep suffering, let's look at two different ways of relating to suffering.

There is a fundamental difference between you having physical, mental, and emotional discomfort or even pain, and these things having you. In the first case, you are aware of the discomfort but remain objective and in charge of managing it. In the second, you feel robbed of your power, either by the cause of the discomfort or by the discomfort itself. This is very frustrating. It makes you feel unhappy, probably angry, and certainly not in charge of the situation. When you feel like this, it's automatic to look for people or things to blame.

People whose feelings fit with the second scenario are victims to both the cause of the suffering and to the way they feel. They feel trapped with no way out. Unfortunately, this can be a longstanding pattern of thinking, feeling, and reacting for many people. However, there is a way out. There is another way of being that may not end the problem responsible for the suffering but will reduce the frustration, hopelessness, and unhappiness caused by it.

Putting an end to Suffering That Isn't Extreme

The first point here is to realize that the feeling of suffering is always a call to action. There is no point in just putting up with suffering: do something about it. If you take on this message, you will be unstoppable!

The way to put an end to (non-extreme) suffering can be stated quite simply:

- Stop focusing on what you don't want.

- Decide what you do want.

- Decide what actions are needed to achieve it.

- Take action on what you do want.

Here's an example. Somebody drives into your car, causing thousands of dollars' worth of damage. Society would regard this as a typical "victim" situation—newspapers would report that "the victim was lucky to walk away without injuries."

How would somebody who is a victim be in this situation? That person would be angry and could well be crying—the upset would be overwhelming. That person's focus would be on his or her loss.

How would somebody who is not a victim be in this situation? He or she certainly wouldn't be happy about it but would nevertheless be organizing an exchange of insurance information, calling the police, and working out how he or she was going to be carless for as short a time as possible. That person's focus would be on managing the situation so he or she could get back to having his or her life back to normal as soon as possible.

It's not hard to see which of these two approaches is more successful and more effective.

Eliminate Victim Thinking

Here are some practical things to do to get rid of the habits that are responsible for being a victim. If you use these consistently, before long, you will be able to look back and be amazed that you could ever have bought into the role of victim.

1. *Don't be a self-critic.* If your internal chatterbox starts to criticize you, interrupt that thought. That's all it is, a repetitive, automatic thought. To start with, it isn't true. Think about something happy and move on. Ignore self-critical thoughts. Practise this forever, if it should take that long. It won't though; your subconscious mind will get the message after a while, and self- critical thoughts will start to disappear.

2. *Interrupt yourself before you react with upset.* Think about people and situations in which you get upset, and identify how you respond. Do you shout angrily, burst into tears, walk away in a huff, say nothing, and then stew over what they said and what you wish you had said?

   Plan ahead. Make a list of the people and situations that (you have allowed to) trigger upsets. Next to each person or situation, write down your usual responses—crying, swearing at them, or arguing, for instance.

   Arrange one or more practice sessions in which you take on being an actor, acting how you will handle these people or situations in a way that enables you to stay in charge of yourself. Prepare a script as if you are writing a play or a movie.

   - Start with what the other person said (or might say) that would usually upset you.

   - Pretend you are in charge—perhaps even pretend you are someone who always stays positive and never gets trapped in situations. Write down what that person would think and then what they would say about the hurtful comment.

   - Practise what you would say to the other person, something calm that would not upset him or her.

   Acting a role like this will feel very odd and difficult at first, but if you keep practising, you will become calm and confident in the face of criticism and anger. If you just don't make any progress, or if you have really difficult emotional issues, consider getting help with this from a counsellor.

3. *Identify other things you can do.* Use the list you created in the previous item (item two). In each situation or for each person, put down a list of bullet points identifying a different interpretation

you could put on the situation or person that would make you feel empowered. Choose a different and more effective way you could be next time. For instance

- you could be someone who is confident, successful, and caring;

- you could be someone who doesn't get caught up with small-minded thinking and talking; or

- you could be someone who is happy and relaxed and who sees the best in people.

You can also use the method I used in chapter 5 to deal with my reaction to certain people getting angry with me. In brief, I invoked my Higher Self and also used my "three words." That was in the section "Direct Your Thoughts and Feelings." You may want to re-read that section.

Decide which of these strategies appeals to you, and create your own formula for success. Get into the habit of repeating whichever exercise(s) you choose as soon as possible after finding yourself in the victim mode.

4. *Identify what you most want.* Make it a habit to remember to ask yourself, "What did I most want in that situation?" whenever you have a problem or something goes wrong. This is the question that a successful person asks. Don't struggle to find the answer. Just search your heart; what you want will be something simple.

Here's an example—a true story about my friend, Glenda. Her daughter, Jess, and Jess's boyfriend, John, got engaged. His parents decided to celebrate with a family dinner party. Glenda, who was single and wasn't very confident in party situations with people she didn't know, was invited. She arrived, had a couple of drinks, and then the meal started.

Things were going well, but gradually, people got noisy and less inhibited. John's mother started picking on Jess, giving her a hard time about something. This really annoyed Glenda, but she didn't say anything. Finally, the noise and John's mother's behaviour got to her, and she exploded. She told John's mother just what she thought of her and stormed out.

The next morning, she realized what she had done. She was going to run into these people at every family function for years and years, and they would be as awkward with her as she felt with them. What a mess she had created!

Where did Glenda go wrong? She focused on the upsetting situation, not on what she wanted. If she had only asked herself, "What do I most want here?" it could have gone so much better. She would have realized that she was tired, couldn't hear properly because of all the noise, and wasn't enjoying herself. What she most wanted was to get home ASAP. She could have excused herself and left. Problem solved. Unfortunately, Glenda allowed her junior autopilot to take over, and it reacted very negatively (through her). If her conscious, able-to-choose mind had stayed in charge, she would have handled the situation sensibly (and maturely).

5. *Don't take it personally!* Life isn't personal, even when it *really* feels like it is.

Let's think about some of the big things that happen to people. When a major event occurs, we usually judge it as good or bad. However, we are never really in a position to judge. The "bad" experience could bring us the greatest learning of our lives. It may result in a life-altering insight or open up a life-altering, fabulous future. Paralympic athletes show us how shattering disabilities can be transformed into golden opportunities. If we stay focused on the bad aspect of events and what we have lost, we may never get to see the potential benefits hidden behind the outer appearance. Always remain open to unseen possibilities; actively look for them in unfamiliar directions.

It is easy to fall into the trap of taking it personally when other people are very unpleasant to us. However, you don't have to buy into their blame or whatever else they are trying to communicate. They are "doing their thing" on the basis of the information and degree of expertise that they possess. They may not possess much of either, and they probably don't if they are attacking you. Stay outside of their upset. Be an outside observer of their performance.

Let's analyse what we are doing if we take it personally when people are critical of us, directly or indirectly. We are allowing (a) someone else's opinion to (b) activate our pride or our judging habit, so we (c) react by feeling the need to defend the immature, vulnerable part of ourselves. This is an autopilot reaction, not a mindful, well-thought-out choice.

Does anyone else's opinion really matter? It only matters if we decide that it is giving us a new insight—one that helps us to change our own thinking. We can only decide this if we remain objective—mentally get outside the problem or situation. Then we are able to spot any elements of truth that we want to take on board.

What is pride, and do we need to boost our self-importance? Taking personal pride in doing something well could be considered appropriate. However, if we are doing something well for its own sake, pride really doesn't come into it. If we are doing something well to impress someone else, we are setting ourselves up for potential disappointment. I think you will agree that pride and the need to boost one's own self-importance are negative rather than positive impulses. Pride and self-importance just get in the way. Love, humility, and contributing generously for no special reason are so much more powerful as ways of being.

If you are creating now with these as your gold standard, you won't take things personally; it will be almost impossible to be a victim.

6. *Lighten up. Be happy. Always be mindful of the big picture.* The big picture is your whole lifetime. If you are a visual person, you might like to try projecting yourself into space where you can look down on planet Earth from your own viewing platform. How does the situation look from up there? Most likely, the problem will shrink in importance. Think about it. Aren't there are always plenty of reasons to be happy? Make being happy your top priority!

Managing More Extreme Suffering

We can't always avoid experiencing suffering, but we can reduce its impact. Here are some thoughts about how to do this.

1. *Take care of yourself.* Whether the cause of the suffering is primarily physical, mental, or emotional, it's important to take care of yourself when you are immersed in it. Don't use suffering to give yourself permission to take part in harmful behaviours, like drinking alcohol, overeating, or driving aggressively. Taking care of yourself means nurturing your way through to the better times that are ahead. Keep reminding yourself that better times *are* ahead.

    Mostly, we don't think of ourselves as our own personal caregivers. It's not something that most people are able to do consistently or do well. However, it is a most important skill to have, and to use. Some may judge this as being selfish, weird, or unnecessary, but they are wrong. When you injure your body and don't take responsibility for taking care of the injury, complications or permanent loss of function are likely. The same is true of emotional injuries.

Did I say mollycoddle yourself? No, and that's not what I am suggesting. Take note when you are hurt. Don't just tough it out, cry it out, or anger it out and hope it will go away. Look through this chapter and follow the suggestions here. There are several. If you follow them, you will heal the hurt so it doesn't persist as another layer of inner resistance in your subconscious mind.

2. *Get some perspective on the situation.*

- Is the problem mild, moderate, or severe? There's a big difference between having a broken leg, a chronic cough, or an upsetting argument, on the one hand, and a monumental problem, on the other.

- Is the problem temporary or permanent? If it's temporary, how long are you willing to put up with it before doing whatever it takes to solve it? If it's permanent, how long are you willing to put up with it as it is now before doing whatever it takes to improve it?

3. *Suffering is not the enemy.* This may seem to be a strange thing to say. However, it points to the fact that we mostly resist having pain. It seems natural to do so. However, remember the saying, "What you resist persists." I am keen that you don't have to experience suffering, or if you do, that it's for as short a time as possible. Resisting the experience of suffering, judging it to be bad, and giving way to negative emotional reactions is absolutely habitual for some people. Sadly, it locks them into more and more suffering.

As I said earlier, being able to think outside of the suffering offers a better way of managing the experience. What can you do?

- *Breathe into the pain itself.* When you stretch a painful muscle, it helps enormously to pretend you are actually breathing through the painful area. There are two disciplines here. The first is being with the pain, and the second is directing the experience of breathing into the painful area. Do I know how this works? No. Does it matter? No. Does it help? Yes!

- *Focus on breathing.* Focus on the feeling of your chest expanding and contracting. Feel the flow of air through your nostrils; breathe through your nostrils rather than your mouth. Calm the rate and depth of your breathing; get it under control. Make it calm and relaxed—stress free. Carry this intention into your mind, and let your thoughts be relaxed.

- *Become aware of other sensations of resistance in your body.* When we are in the midst of suffering and resisting, our bodies reflect it. We may clench our jaws or our fists or tighten the stomach muscles. Muscle-tension headaches are a common accompaniment. Feel what's happening inside your body, and breathe through any areas that are mirroring your mental or emotional discomfort. Allow your body to relax. Bring thoughts of caring and love to your whole body.

Fighting is never a successful solution to anything. Peace is the natural order. We only have to remove what's in the way, and peace will be present. Our job, then, is to identify what's in the way and then create and manage the solutions. The problem is that we mostly resist and look for shortcuts. Allow yourself to feel all the feelings and the sensations and to know this is the way things are for right now. By doing so, you make it possible to experience peace.

4. *In extremis.* Extreme suffering is terrible for all concerned. Cancer-related pain and acute major trauma require actions in addition to those listed in the previous sections. The key is to identify the cause of the problem and to address that—keeping going until the suffering has been alleviated or at least brought down to a manageable degree.

An unexpected death may cause extreme emotional suffering. The support of others is often the most helpful remedy here. The process of grieving is well understood, and professional help should be sought if the suffering is incapacitating or too prolonged.

Extreme suffering is a major topic—or rather, a series of specialized topics. If you need help, consider seeing a trained professional or obtaining reading material specific to the cause of the suffering.

Positive Aspects of Suffering

Are there any positives in suffering? When you are caught up in the suffering, right in the middle of the whole unpleasant emotional flow, this question is irrelevant. It will only make you more upset. Think about this question when the emotional heat has lessened and you can think with more objectivity.

Yes, there are positive aspects to suffering.

- *Suffering offers an opportunity to learn.* If we can step outside the upset of the suffering and look at what we could have done to avoid what happened, we can often learn valuable life lessons. We may decide to be more prudent with investing, choosing "value investing" with long-term profitability rather than short-term, high-profit, high-risk investing. We may realize that we have a problem with anger that we need to address, or that we've put up with others' dysfunctional behaviour instead of being assertive. In chapter 19, we will be talking about things that trigger us into becoming upset. Identifying our emotional triggers and then working on these bring fabulous personal growth. Insights about how we can improve our performance are invaluable, provided we then follow through, learn, and improve how we do things.

- *Suffering is often the initiator of change.* Often, people put up with suboptimal conditions because they are too lazy to change, because the conditions are familiar, because they procrastinate, or because of other priorities. It's only when the degree of suffering becomes intolerable that they do something about their conditions; then they find a way to make things change.

  We see this in public, corporate, and private life. It's sometimes the reason why there is a change of government, a change of leadership, a divorce, or why someone might move away from flat mates. Change always opens the door to new opportunities. Whether we make the most of those opportunities is up to us.

- *Suffering activates the heart.* When a natural disaster causes suffering, we see the best come out in people. Deep down, we care for other people, and when they are in need, we are moved. We may be on the other side of the world, but love and concern move us to donate money, time, or goods to those needing help. Our prayers are with them too. Perhaps re-read the touching quotation at the start of this chapter attributed to Mother Teresa.

It is true that we can become desensitised to traumatic incidents by repeatedly seeing scenes of suffering on our TV screens. However, if we notice we are not moved by such things, we need to identify that as a signal that we are on autopilot. Bring those people into living reality instead of thinking of them as theoretical concepts, and immediately, we are moved. Watching suffering acted out as entertainment is putting negative messages into our minds.

Choose to watch programmes and movies that are uplifting. There is more on this subject in chapter 14, in the section "Choose What You Allow into Your Mind."

Caring for others is the most valuable aspect of our humanity. Developing this in ourselves enhances the quality of all life and the quality of all consciousness on our planet.

Is There a Relationship Between Current and Past Suffering?

Several writers distinguish two subtypes of suffering or pain: current pain and pain from the past that is still "trapped" in the mind or body. Some even go so far as to say that the emotional suffering we experience is a reactivation of past, unresolved emotional pain. If this is true, then resolving past issues may be extremely important. I don't pretend to be a psychologist or psychotherapist, and therefore, I don't plan to discuss this further. If you would like to investigate this line of thinking, perhaps with a view to "healing the past," I recommend Michael Brown's book, *The Presence Process*[1].

Let me remind you that we will be returning to the subject of suffering but from a different perspective in the last chapter.

Summary

1. Some suffering is the result of being in the role of victim. It takes effort to get out of this habit, but the good news is that it can be achieved once you identify the problem and then do what it takes to eliminate it. Not indulging in blame or feeling sorry for yourself is an excellent place to start.

2. If you find yourself suffering, stop focusing on (and talking about) what you don't want. Instead, focus and take action on what you do want.

3. Allow your problems to exist rather than automatically resisting them with thoughts like, *It shouldn't be like this!* Allowing them does not mean you don't do anything about them.

4. Manage your problems: don't ignore them or resist them. If you don't know how to manage a problem that's causing suffering, get help and get on with sorting it out.

5. Manage your sense of self: don't let self-importance sabotage your ability to think, or trick you into reacting.

6. Take good care of yourself at all times. Keep the problem causing the suffering in perspective.

7. If you are suffering, life is offering you an opportunity. It's a call to be in action, and it's an opportunity for insight.

Practice

1. Switch on your mental radar so it notifies you when you are about to take something personally.

When it alerts you to a situation in which there's a risk of reacting, interrupt any automatic thoughts and feelings by deciding, "I am not reacting here. I am free to think about this and free to choose what to think, say, and do next!"

2. Practise the strategies shown in the section "Eliminate Victim Thinking."

3. Practise the actions shown in the Summary section.

4. Spend time thinking about the situations and people that seem to be the cause your suffering, and make notes.

- Create new ways of looking at them.

- Create new beliefs about yourself: you are a successful, creative person.

- You can create advantages out of adversity. Make doing this a project that you work on frequently.

5. If you have recurrent upset and persistent suffering, this is a sign that there are important areas where healing is required. Start by identifying those areas, either by yourself or with the help of a counsellor. Then you can begin the task of healing past memories and past trauma and move towards a healthier, happier future.

Reference

[1] Brown, M. (2010). *The Presence Process*. Revised Edition. Vancouver, Canada: Namaste Publishing.

PART III

ORGANIZED FOR SUCCESS

CHAPTER 13

SYSTEMS THAT WORK

> I pulled out box after box, setting them haphazardly around the room. My organization lacked something—like, say, organization.
> —Rachael Mead

Build on Your Successes

Excitement and enthusiasm are wonderful feelings. The energy from them seems to give us extra powers and often leads to unexpected results. When experiencing them, you get more done with seemingly less time or effort.

Times like these are opportunities to build on your success—to take more ground. Your next area for achievement doesn't have to be related to whatever led to you to feel on top of the world. You might set a new goal or pick an existing goal on which to focus your super drive. You are the best one to decide how to use your newfound energy and enthusiasm. The main thing is to make sure you recognize that your highs are opportunities and to use them to transport you to even more success.

I mention this point because people who are not fully organized in the ways discussed below often feel inner resistance to getting organized. It's best to do the following work when you are feeling energetic, inspired, and ready to tackle a challenge that will really help you move forward.

Are You Properly Organized?

One of the main difficulties we all face in our busy lives is the problem of achieving balanced lives—or more accurately, fully integrated lives. There are so many things to do, so many demands on our time and energy; it can be very difficult to manage every aspect of life. However, it's not impossible. Being organized is the starting point. There are seven aspects to being organized:

- Identify the various aspects of your life; keep working on all of them, not just your favourites.

- Know what you value.

- Have goals.

- Plan ahead; use monthly and weekly task lists.

- Know and see what you are managing.

- Keep written records; this is the only way you can keep track of what you are up to and what stages have been reached in all the things you are managing.

- Organize your time.

This chapter looks at all of these aspects except for goals. They are discussed in chapter 16.

Roles Help You Keep an Eye on Your Whole Life

The word *roles* refers to different activity areas of your life. I'm sure the activities in your role at work are quite different from those in your role at home, from your financial role, and from your health and fitness role, for example. Our degrees of organization and our expectations of ourselves are also often very different in our various roles.

Life gets out of balance, or disintegrates, when you give a great deal of attention to certain roles and practically none to others. This imbalance isn't healthy. It means there some aspects of life where you are taking little or no responsibility. You know what happens when you take your eye off the ball: eventually you drop it. In other words, ignoring parts of your life is risky. On the other hand, the chances of having a successful, satisfying life increase astronomically if you actively manage all your roles. This doesn't have to be hard work. The minimum requirement is to pay attention to each role every week. Even if you have given some responsibilities to your spouse, a business partner, or even your cleaner, make sure you keep track of what's happening in those areas.

Create a List of Your Roles

When you start listing your roles, you may find the list starts off being very long. However, the aim is to end up with about seven roles. You will need to combine some. For instance, in your "people" role, you could combine family and friends.

Your initial list of roles might look something like this:

    family and friends

    my job

    health and fitness

finances

self-improvement

relaxation

my environment

Great Names Make a Difference

The next step is to create names that give you inspiration: don't put up with boring names for your roles. For example, the roles in the list above might be renamed as follows:

fabulous family and friends

super mum, rocketing sales, or legal eagle, etc.

golden-goose care. (This term reflects the fact that you are like the golden goose in Grimm's fairy tales. The moral of that story is that it is important to look after the golden goose, not take it for granted.)

money magnet/multi-millionaire

continuous improvement

lifestyle, leisure, and fun

amazing environments

Feel free to use these names if you like, but ideally you should be creative; take your time and create your own.

Mission Statements for Roles

You should probably move on from this particular exercise, and come back later when you have time to write a short mission statement for each role. Here are some ideas:

- Donna and I wrote this poetic one when we decided to be in a permanent relationship more than twenty years ago:

  Synergistic partnership,

  Sensual and cerebral,

  Playful and adventurous—

  A springboard for amazing lives.

- Then there's my health and fitness mission statement:

  Fit, firm, and flexible,

  Trim, taut, and terrific,

  Till the day I drop into my box!

A mission statement needs to be interesting, inspiring, and concise. If you can't remember it easily, it's not a winner.

Synergy between Roles

One of the big benefits of having a well-established system of roles is that the more you work with this system, the more you are going to find synergy happening between the various aspects of your life. Synergy, as you know, is when the result is greater than the sum of the parts. As an example, I regularly find synergy in the form of unexpected benefits and happy coincidences between three of my roles that are closely aligned: continuous improvement, champion of Qabalah and life coach entrepreneur. I frequently find that synergy also flowing into my medical practice, inspiring me to contribute effectively to patients who are facing upsetting problems and difficulties.

Success in one area of life can energize other areas. This is probably the simplest and most frequently experienced example of synergy between roles. Once you start looking, you will see synergy in action in your own life. It is exciting and really satisfying.

Using Your Roles

Managing your whole life is only possible if you consider each area regularly. Shortly, we are going to talk about having a weekly task list and a monthly task list. Not everyone needs these, but busy people do—otherwise important matters get forgotten. I use my list of roles as the basis for deciding what I want to complete each week and each month. I also use it to set up goals in most parts of my life every year.

Please let me know if you would like help in getting this system working (adrian@SpinDoctor.com).

See What You Are Managing—Use a Whiteboard

Busy people usually have multiple projects happening. Some are big, some small, but all are important. It can seem like life is one big juggling act, with enormous upset waiting to kick-in if you drop just one ball. Retrieving the dropped ball takes a lot of effort, and that can threaten your whole act.

The only way to manage your way easily through a busy life is to keep a record of everything you are managing at any one time. A mind map is a great way to keep an overview of all your activities. Ideally you would also have separate mind maps for each of your busiest roles. The advantage of a mind map is that it is a picture whose structure is imprinted in nature and in our own nervous systems. If you are not familiar with mind mapping, check it out online.

My favourite way of doing this is on a whiteboard in my office. On a whiteboard you can easily make changes as often as needed. On my whiteboard summary, I have an easily visible, written record that shows me what I am managing and where I am. You could also do this on your computer: OneNote (in Microsoft Office) is a fantastic system for managing anything.

Know When to Delegate and When to Dismiss

Knowing when to delegate or dismiss is a crucial part of being properly organized. *Managing* does not mean "doing everything yourself." If life is overwhelming you, give priority to asking, "Do I really need to do this?"

Perhaps there are some activities that you felt you needed to do in the past but that are no longer necessary. The tasks you do to tidy up after your family or that you do because no one else wants to do them are good places to look. This is not an invitation to lower your standards, however! I recommend improving standards through improved organization. Just as it's important to look through your wardrobe and remove clothing you no longer use, it's important to look through your life and remove tasks and people that are no longer appropriate.

Doing everything yourself and continually suffering is a sure sign that you are cut off from the people in your life. Stop suffering. Bring in the people you know.

- Make appropriate requests.

- Ask them if they know reliable people who could help.

- Make enjoying and contributing to the people in your life a priority. Making requests of them is a way of contributing, provided it is appropriate and occasional. Overusing friends is a sure way of losing them.

- Look up sources for help on the Internet.

Be committed to happiness and finding solutions. Don't condemn yourself to suffering.

Planning Is Essential

Always have a plan. Plan today. Plan this week. Plan this month. Plan this year. Plan your long-term future too.

Earlier in this chapter, we looked at our roles in life. These all need plans. How wealthy do you want to be in two, five, and ten years' time? What's your plan for creating that? How do you want your marriage, your health, and the rest of your life to look at these times and beyond? You need a plan so that you will achieve those things too.

What is a plan? Plans always involve actions; they are not wish lists, and they are not orders. If you are not taking actions to get what you want, it won't happen. Visualizing success at doing things is a particular action, and it definitely helps. However, taking action in the real world is absolutely essential. Plans show the steps to your goals; they include strategically organized actions, thought out and written down before you start doing those tasks.

Plans need to be flexible. Unforeseen opportunities and problems are bound to occur. (Actually, they are *all* opportunities.) A most important principle in making plans and in pursuing goals is to be intentional but unattached to the outcomes.

When you remain unattached to the exact outcome, you are open to other possibilities. Your purposeful intentions and your desire for success send a particular vibration into the universal subconsciousness. However, there may be other benefits that you are also attracting, perhaps through your desire to help others, for example. Don't get in the universe's way by holding a rigid, fixed picture of the results you are drawing towards yourself. Stay open to the universal beneficence and abundance that is always operating outside your awareness.

Managing Tasks With a Weekly Task List

Managing your life from day to day and week to week isn't rocket science. All you need to do is to make the commitment and be in action. The best way I know of doing this is to create and use a weekly task list that includes the following:

- the days of the week

- tasks and appointments that you choose for each day, including the weekend

- must-do items, identified and prioritized (Your PPIs - potential procrastination items from chapter nine will be included in these.)

Make sure the must-do items get done on a given day, no matter what else happens that day.

How to Use a Weekly Task List

- Create a new list at the same time every week. Sunday is the day I choose for this. Include the phone numbers of people you need to call. If you also have a monthly task list completed, using this makes it very quick and easy to create your weekly task list.

- Look at the weekly task list every morning before starting any other work. Prioritize the tasks for that day by numbering them in order of importance. Decide whether some of them need to be performed at a particular time.

- Now do all the tasks that have not already been allocated to another time, in order of priority.

- As the days and week progress, other tasks will show up. Add them to the appropriate section of your weekly task list or to your monthly task list.

Use a Monthly Task List Too

I also have a monthly task list on which I list everything I want to or need to complete that month. As you would expect, I check my PPI list and make sure those items are included.

Here's how to organize your monthly task list:

- Create a list of the roles or various activities in your life.

- Under each role, list any recurring activities that are important to get done each month—things like paying your credit cards and bills—or particular family members or friends with whom you want to keep in contact.

- Include birthdays and appointments, as well as general tasks.

- Under each role, write down the name of the goals or projects that you have for that role. Now decide what tasks you want to complete for each of these this month.

- Strike through the items you complete. You can still read them, but they are obviously completed.

I make sure my whiteboard has up-to-date goals, projects, and tasks. Sure, there is some overlap between my whiteboard summary and the weekly and monthly lists. That's okay.

Update your monthly task list and whiteboard every week when you do your weekly planning.

Organize Your Time

Things that need to be scheduled are mentioned throughout this book. You need your own list, but let me suggest some important items:

- *planning time*—the time in which business owners work on the business, not in the business; time spent working on your goals and projects, identifying the next steps, but not doing tasks; time spent doing some research; and time spent arranging your weekly and monthly tasks lists

- *personal focus time*—choosing your being; connecting with "yourself at your best"; meditation

- *personal development time*—reading, analysing problems, updating your success diary

- *relaxation and rejuvenation time*—no tasks here, just enjoyment

- *exercise time*

- *housework and general tasks*

- *people time*—time for socializing and staying in communication

Keep a Success Diary

A success diary isn't an essential item, but it's one I highly recommend. There are different ways of going about it. You can track your main successes every month, or you can track your successes in every role every week.

The reason for keeping a success diary is that it brings your successes up to a conscious level. Often, particularly if you are very busy, you can go from one task to the next without taking a moment to recognize the significance of what you have achieved. When this happens every day, massive amounts of success evaporate from consciousness. The potential energy from being highly satisfied is not accessed. It disappears underfoot as we push ourselves along the treadmill of busyness.

Even if you just keep track of your big successes every week and put these in your success diary, you will be amazed at the end of three months and certainly by the end of the year. You can build on your successes, but only if you acknowledge them at a conscious level. This is what a success diary allows you to do.

Special Memories

Some moments in life have special meaning—they are golden moments. Don't let them slip away. They are invaluable in their own right, but more importantly, you can use them. We all have our own special memories. They might include your wedding day, the birth of a child, fabulous holidays, the achievement of a goal you worked long and hard to achieve, an unexpected honour, a reconciliation, family events, and more.

These days it's easy to take photos, and you could keep a special-memories photo file. That would be ideal. But there may be no photos of some special moments, so take the time to write down a list. Include notes that help bring the full picture and the feelings into focus. Schedule the time to do this soon. Talk about those times with the people involved and really bring those moments to life once more. Your list and photo file will become more valuable as time goes by. Make sure yours are up to date.

We started this chapter by saying that highs from our successes can fuel future progress. Special memories from previous years can also be used for this purpose. Later in this book, I will show you another way to get value from your special memories.

Summary

1. Highs that result from successes are opportunities; use that energy, that enthusiasm, to take you to even more success.

2. Managing your whole life is only possible if you consider each area regularly. Your list of roles is a framework for organizing your life.

3. When you work with your roles to plan tasks and to identify your successes, life becomes very connected and very satisfying. This is the way to go from mediocrity to excellence, from an ordinary life to an extraordinary one, from "doing okay" to enjoying success after success.

4. Your key tools:

- a whiteboard or a computer-based equivalent

- your list of roles

- a weekly task list

- a monthly task list

- your success diary (optional but highly recommended)

With these, you can keep your life under your gaze at a conscious level. You won't rely on memory or hope. You can keep yourself on track and plan ahead. It isn't hard. It will take some time and energy for a few months, but then it will be automatic and easy.

Use your imagination to make implementing this enjoyable. Chart your successes, and be challenged by any setbacks. Being organized is your ticket to an amazing future!

Practice

There is more than enough material in the text of this chapter to guide you. How great—there are no extra homework tasks. My advice: schedule the time to work on this material, and incorporate the practices in this chapter into your way of doing things.

CHAPTER 14

YOUR IDEAL LIFE—THE LIFE OF YOUR DREAMS

> Dream lofty dreams, and as you
> dream, so shall you become.
> —James Allen

Little children are very special. In their age of innocence, they move between living in the real world and living in the world of their dreams. They lose themselves zooming a small car around, perhaps imagining themselves speeding along, performing amazing driving feats. Well, that's a boy thing, but girls do exactly the same. Whether it's chanting as they skip with a skipping rope, playing hide and seek, or playing with dolls, children have a wonderful ability to live in a world of imagination. Can you remember any of your dream worlds from when you were very young?

Breaking Free of a Limiting Reality

As adults, we often get so busy in our own "real worlds" and get so used to living with time, financial, work, and family constraints that we stop using our "play vision." We lose our ability to live for a while in a world of our dreams. We get used to coping with things like the rigors of bringing up a family with limited resources, and putting up with a feeling of isolation from others because we have to continually push ourselves on the treadmill of life.

Of course, this statement doesn't apply to everyone. Many people have the exactly opposite experience—time hangs heavily on their hands, and boredom is one of the crosses they bear through life.

The point I am making is that, to many people, life is an experience of some sort of limitation. They feel stuck, to varying degrees, with the present physical reality, and if there is a way out, it seems like it's over a very distant horizon.

The tragedy is that this will indeed be true if you hang on to these thoughts and beliefs. However, if you use the training given previously in this book, you will realize that thoughts are just thoughts, and you know that you can change your thoughts. With old, well-established thought habits, you need to be alert and notice when they are present; then you can quickly dismiss and replace them. We are only trapped in limitation if we allow ourselves to be.

Make a promise to yourself: "I won't allow myself to do nothing when I feel stuck." Instead

- identify what you want, use your imagination, and focus on the feelings of having it;

- look around your life and find evidence that you already have what you want in some way and to some extent;

- keep looking for more evidence day after day and be grateful;

- keep bringing your attention to loving what it is that you want as if you already have it, knowing that in doing so you are creating a pathway with your thoughts and feelings to having it.

There's more to do, so keep reading. But you have begun moving along your path to freedom.

Dreams

In this chapter, when I use the words *dream* or *dreams*, I am not referring to the dreams we have when we are asleep. I am referring to ideas that the conscious mind initiates and allows the subconscious mind to develop. Subconsciousness plays an important role in this because it gives us access to imagination and creativity. However, it is with the conscious part of our minds that we choose the topic about which we dream creatively, the directions we explore, and the outcomes we want.

It's really important to set time aside to dream creatively. Doing this builds flexibility into the thoughts we think, helps us be more creative in our daily life, and helps reduce stress and the need to use force in order to get what we want. The freedom we feel while dreaming creatively becomes available in our real world.

Dream Your Way Into a New Vision

When I started writing this chapter, I quickly realized that I was writing advice and instructions for myself, as well as for the good people reading this book. I have worked hard all my life, and as I am writing this, I am still working hard to transition from working as a doctor into being a highly successful author, life coach, and coaching entrepreneur. It's time for me to get off the treadmill or, more accurately, to get rid of the thoughts about hard work, effort, and struggle, and focus fully on enjoying the process of becoming even more successful in my new career than I have been as a doctor.

Writing has always been one of my passions, so I am on the right path. However, what I am still learning and practising is expanding the dream of my new career into a vision—one in which I am living as a fabulously rich and famous author, coach, and entrepreneur.

Let's explore the transitioning process. You can then start it immediately.

As I have said so many times before, the journey starts when you decide what you want. My youngest daughter, Julie, had twin girls a month before I started this chapter. She already had two boys, almost five and three years old respectively. Before she became pregnant with the twins, she was painting regularly and developing her unique style as an artist. She and her husband had just moved into a very small house in suburban Auckland. Perhaps her dream vision might be to really enjoy being a wonderfully successful wife and mum *and* to have the time and space to paint regularly and become a very successful artist.

You can immediately see the physical limitations she faces. However, in the world of your dreams, you can remove whatever limitations you choose. Okay, if you have an artificial limb, you can't grow a new one, but that limb doesn't need to limit your success or happiness. In the world of your dreams, you have access to the limitless abundance of the universe. You can make over any aspects of your appearance. You have unlimited funds. You can travel where and when you want, live where you want. You can enjoy life and be immensely happy.

What you want may be a mystery when you start this process. However, just start with the small stuff: a happy home, a healthy body, good food, and good friends. Get these sorts of ideals in place in your mind and written down.

What's next? Perhaps choosing a job—no, let's say a career—that you would love. Perhaps your dream position would be as a hairdresser, a manager of a retail store, a physicist, or an Olympic athlete. Choose something that seems realistic, even if it would stretch you; make sure you choose what would absolutely delight you.

What else? Do you want to travel? Okay, write down a list of the places you want to visit. Prioritize them. Julie might put gorgeous places around New Zealand and Australia at the top of her list, saving more distant locations until travel with (or without) her children is easier and the mortgage on the larger house she envisions having is under control.

Gradually, you build up a picture of what you want, writing it down so you can read it frequently. In this way, you are keeping it at the front of your mind.

Keep the Dream Or Vision Alive

Creating a dream is not a one-off exercise. Like a plant growing indoors, you need to visit it, feed and water it, enjoy it, love it, and keep it alive. If you pay attention to it and look after it, it will grow. Your ideas will expand, and they will grow even more beautiful and inspiring. Your dream can and should be a fabulous inner oasis that not only brings you enormous pleasure before it begins to manifest but also alters your life as it gradually becomes the life of your dreams.

How do you keep the dream alive and grow the dream? Several ways to do this are listed in chapter 17, in the section "Creating Supports for Your Intentions." Rather than repeat that information here, I want to discuss another important part of the process of living the dream.

Forget About *How*: Let the Universe Manage the Hows

Creative dreams are not goals, although they may become goals if you so choose and when you are ready. But at the dream stage, you do not have to get caught up in how to close the gap between the present and your ideal future. This is not your job. Leave this to the universe.

At the dream stage, your job has three parts:

- You must feel and see yourself living your dream.

- If it really is your ideal, you will feel inspired by it. You will automatically think about it.

- Be alert and awake to the opportunities the universe brings. They will move you towards living your dream.

By doing these things, you are sending particular vibrations out into the universal subconsciousness. Provided there is no ambivalence, no conflicting thoughts and feelings about what you want, you will eventually attract the people and the circumstances that manifest your desires.

The path towards manifesting your dream may well take directions you cannot envisage. The universe is happy to handle all the hows that are needed to bring the dream into physical reality. Don't get in its way. Live like it's happening. One day, it may turn into a project or goal, like my new career, and you will be motivated to take courses, learn new skills, and put time and money into making it happen. Allow your dreams to develop.

Summary

1. Dreams of something better do not thrive if you are focused on what's wrong in life, how hard or unfair life is, or how stuck you feel.

2. Look beyond the present situation. Our views of life are terribly narrow; we never see the whole picture. Expect more of yourself. Look for reasons to be grateful and happy and expect success.

3. Make the time to dream creatively. Make it a regular part of your schedule. In business, they talk about working *on* your business, not just *in* your business. That's how to make your business take off. It's the same in life: when you keep using your imagination to expand your vision of what's possible in your life, your life takes off!

4. Creative dreams—your vision of exciting possibilities—are invigorating. Your level of enthusiasm jumps up several notches as your excitement and interest grow. These and other benefits spill over into your whole life.

5. Keep your dreams at the front of your mind; write them down, read them, and refine them frequently.

6. Let the universe do its magic. Your job is to keep the vision alive and to take advantage of opportunities when they appear. They don't just appear, though; you are attracting them by the positive focus of your thoughts and feelings.

Practice

1. Do you have dreams of your future life that excite you? If so, write the story of what you are doing, feeling, and enjoying and the new opportunities that have occurred as if you have already manifested your future dream life. Include as many details as possible. Give yourself permission to be really creative as you do this.

2. Are you willing to put half an hour aside this week to play with some ideas?

- Think about the various aspects of your life—the various roles you have. Use them as the starting point for creating some new possibilities that you could have in your life in, say, two to three years' time. They should be things that you are interested in, things that you want. You are not committing to any of them, but do write them down.

- A week later, or sooner if you can, create a new set of possibilities. Then go over your two lists and see which ideas excite and interest you. You might like to do this exercise with a friend and talk about your final list.

- Keep reading your list every week. Refine it as new ideas come along. However, if it's not exciting you, it's probably either because you are very busy, your heart's not in this exercise, or you have not yet identified things that you really want.

Follow the steps shown in this chapter, and you will start moving your life in the direction of your dreams. Patience, persistence, and positive thoughts and feelings will get you there, provided you don't have inner conflict about what you want.

3. The following two exercises are from Marshall Sylver's 1990s book and audio cassette series, *Passion, Profit & Power*. Be imaginative as you design these futures for yourself.

    - Write a description of your ideal work day.

    - Write a description of your ideal day off.

> When you are done, look to see what constraints you have built into these descriptions. Notice where you have carried constraints you are familiar with in today's life—such as time, money or certain people—into your ideal future. Can you relax any of them and create even more wonderful ideal days?
>
> Your ideal days may change as time goes by; feel free to update and improve them.

CHAPTER 15

TARGET WHAT YOU MOST WANT

> As you go through life, make this your goal: keep your eye on the doughnut and not on the hole.
> —Author unknown

Know What You Most Want

Perhaps you have noticed how many times I have already pointed out the importance of knowing what you want. Without any doubt, the first step to success, and the hottest tip in this book, is to know what you want!

The things we most want in our lives change as time goes by. Our desires change as we get experience because experience starts to show us what is possible. Even before we have achieved something important, we often start thinking about what else is possible.

Life is truly a journey. The only question is whether we most want to enjoy the journey or whether we most want just to get somewhere, happy to spend all our time, energy, and emotional energy on that. Actually, you can do both with minimal compromise and with far better results!

Strangely, we are unaware at a conscious level of some of the things that we want, despite the fact that they impact every area of our lives. These things are our values. They operate unseen in the background until you bring them into the awareness of the conscious mind. Then they can be improved and used to your advantage.

The Things About Life That You Value

Values are the qualities of life that we believe are the most important. Values give us our expectations about the way things should be in a perfect world. Also, they determine how we respond to the changing circumstances of life.

There are hundreds of values. While many people in a particular culture may have similar values, each person is unique in how he or she rates or prioritizes his or her own. *Core values* is the term used to describe the top four or five values held by someone.

Identifying Your Values

It is important to identify your values. This is because when you do something that is out of harmony with your core values, the conflict with what you really want (i.e. what your heart says) makes you feel dissatisfied or causes problems. Let's look at examples of how your values can affect you in two areas of your life.

The first area is your home environment. When one of your core values is beauty, buying a home is unlikely to thrill you if you compromise on attractive location, street appeal, and interior appearance just because of the potential for a good return on the investment sometime in the future.

The second area is your relationships. Your ability to get on with others is influenced greatly by values. For instance, a leader's ability to motivate is compromised if his or her values are different from those of the people he or she is meant to be leading, particularly if the leader isn't aware of or ignores the differences. Conflict between different generations of a family is also often the result of conflicting values. For example, teenagers often highly value excitement, while Mum and Dad may instead value security.

You can see how having a good understanding of your values is really important when it comes to choosing your partner—either a business partner or your soul mate. Is he or she really on the same page as you? Better to find out than rely on first impressions, or worse, hope for the best. The excitement of the relationship often makes us want to rush into a commitment we may regret later. Family or friends may see potential problems before we do, although they are more likely to question whether you are really suited for one another than to mention values.

Conflict between Values and Fears

When there is a conflict between your values and your fears, problems and unhappiness are likely to result, as shown by the following opposing value-versus-fear pairs:

> relationship vs. fear of rejection
>
> fame and fortune vs. fear of failure
>
> intimacy vs. fear of commitment

In each instance, avoiding our fears creates a conflict with what we most value. The reverse may also be true: conflict may well occur if we pursue what we most value and ignore our fears. However, in this instance, if we do it with courageous awareness, personal growth may result. An important practice is to periodically compare your list of fears (a.k.a. the things you want to avoid) with your list of values and see if any conflicts exist.

Conflict between Purpose and Values

Let's say you have a goal or purpose. You set about achieving it only to find that your heart isn't in it, and you lose enthusiasm. This can happen because there is a conflict between what you are doing to achieve the goal and your core values.

This happened to me. I was recently drawn into subscribing for software that promised easy money. It was so easy that I should have smelled a rat! But I joined up, paid my money, and then started reading the agreements that were not available until after I had joined. Immediately, I saw that there was a glaring conflict between my purpose in joining—making money without substantial time or effort so I could focus on activities close to my heart—and several of my core values.

Sometimes you can be well into a project and may have completed years of training before the conflict becomes apparent. You will realize the source of your discomfort much faster if you know your core values.

Values Can Change

It's important to review your values periodically, because they can change as a result of experiences. The values you had in your twenties are unlikely to be the same as those you hold in your forties, and those of your forties won't be the same as those you hold in your seventies.

Be Sure You Understand

Values are words, and words can mean different things to different people. The differences may be crucial. For example:

- *Love* might mean "casual caring" or "heartfelt, committed relationship" or "empathy, sympathy or partnership."

- *Spirituality* might mean "altruism," "being in touch with nature spirits," "rigid morality," "academic interest in comparative religion," or "commitment to enlightenment."

It is important to understand your own values and to respect those of the people with whom you have relationships, be they family, friends, or work colleagues.

Again, if you would like help in identifying your own values, please contact me (adrian@SpinDoctor.com). If you would like to read more about values, I recommend *Quantum Leap Thinking* by Richard Mapes[1].

The Excitement of Goals

Because knowing what we want is so important and because having life balance is also important, we are now going to spend time in this chapter targeting our desires across our lives, by setting goals. Then we will look at how to manage those goals, so we get to enjoy our new creations.

Before we go there, however, I want to point out that setting and managing goals doesn't suit everyone. However, setting goals and managing them creates energy. When you go after the things you desire, it's exciting. Hurdles appear, and you work out how to get around them. You grow in knowledge and confidence as you make progress. The more you want it, the greater the benefits that come from focusing on, planning, being, and doing what it takes to get it. Success brings more success. You progress as a person by making it a habit to identify and pursue goals.

Setting Your Goals

There are many ways to go about setting goals, but the following is the one that works, in my experience. There are a number of steps.

1. *Clarify your vision: what do you want to be, do, and have?* Start with the role that most interests you and ask yourself, "What would I most like my life to look like two to three years and, say, five years from now?" (Examples of roles were given in chapter 13.)

   To make it easier, break up this question into smaller questions. Use the following three questions, which are more specific:

   - "What would I most like *to be* in this role two to three years and five years from now?" Answers might include things like "promoted to a higher position in my job," "running my own company," "living with the love of my life," or "stress free and permanently happy," and so on.

   - "What would I most like *to be doing* in this role two to three years and five years from now?"

   - "What would I most like *to have* in this role two to three years and five years from?" The answers may be possessions, skills, assets, or lifestyles, for instance.

   When you have answered these three questions, you will have plenty of information to enable you to write some bullet points or sentences that describe your vision of the future in this role. Eventually, you will do this for each role in turn, but for now, keep going with the one that most interests you.

2. *Start a mind map for each of your roles.* Mind maps have been around for a long time. Assuming you are happy to give mind maps a try, get a pad of A4 paper or use a mind map app on

your computer. The plan is to create a fresh map for each of your roles. However, start with the role that most interests you. Put the name of that role in a circle or a box at the centre of your first role map page. At the top of this page write down the vision you created in step 1.

3. *Add goals to your mind map.* Now it's time to add the goals that will allow you to reach your vision. Each goal will be a new limb radiating out from the role title at the centre of the page.

4. *Add steps to achieving one of your main goals.* These will be branches coming off the limb for that goal. When you are ready, identify the steps to your other goals and add them.

Example: Dave's first mind map for his Acclaimed Musician role.

Vision: I see myself studying for the next four years, and graduating with all the skills I need to support my career as an internationally acclaimed guitarist, song writer, and band leader.

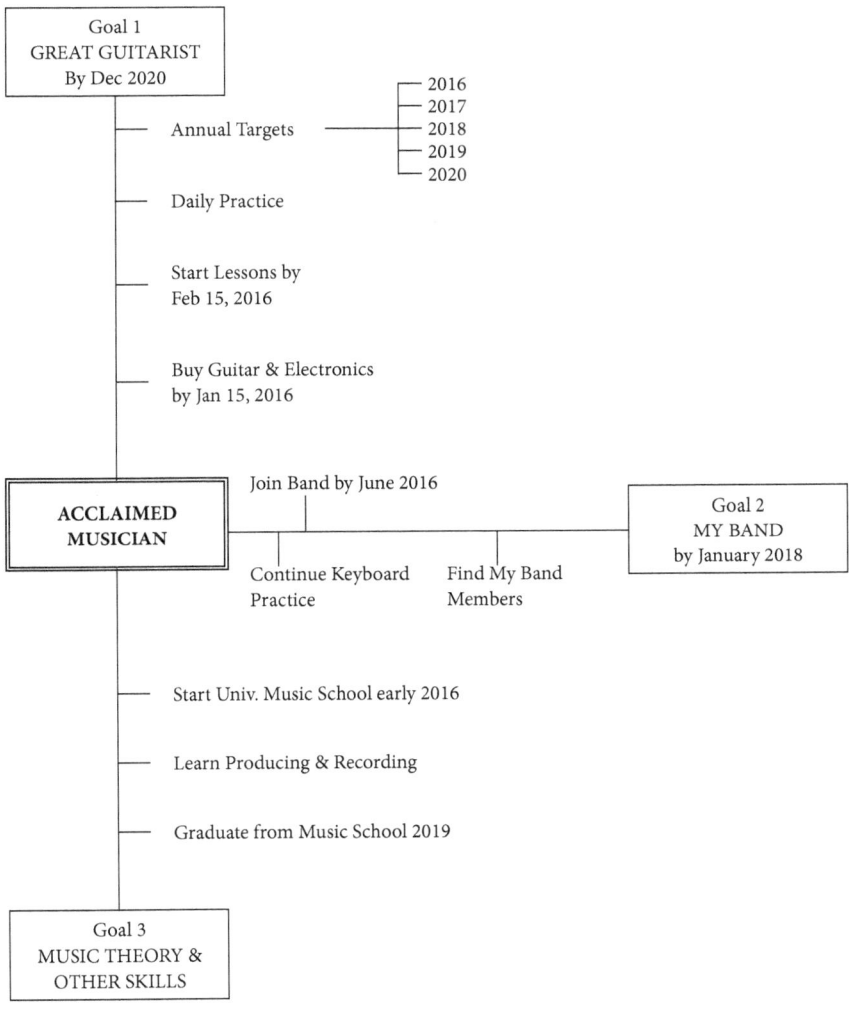

An important aspect of goals is that they have both

- a specific, identifiable result, such as acquiring a new car or a new position in your work; and

- a date by which the goal or sub-goal will have been achieved.

Goals are thus different from aims (such as being happy or being an inspirational role model), which have neither of the two characteristics listed above. There is nothing wrong with having aims, but specific goals are more powerful and call for tangible results.

5. *Let your emotions guide you.* How do you feel as you tackle each role and as you are creating goals? Do you feel excited, really interested, and alive? Or do you feel you are just doing it because you should? Do the goals empower you or disempower you?

Let's say you feel disempowered. If a particular goal *is* what you want, breaking it down into simpler, achievable steps will help you get your enthusiasm back. If, however, there are some goals that elicit negative thoughts or feelings, look at your underlying beliefs. You might find, for example, beliefs like "this is going to be awfully hard work" or "it'll be a miracle if I pull this one off; I've done things like this before and failed."

If this is what your heart and mind are telling you, you have some options. Maybe you need to adjust that goal. Perhaps it isn't what you want to be, do, or have. Or maybe the goal is okay, but you need to get rid of the negative thoughts or beliefs.

Here's how to replace your negative beliefs:

- Create a positive belief, such as "I know I can [fill in the blank] in the next twelve months."

- If that new belief feels unbelievable, adapt it: "I am learning to trust my ability to [fill in the blank] in the next twelve months."

As a bonus step, here, you might create a "My Best Beliefs" page and put your new belief there where you can find it and read it aloud every day.

Are you back on track—enthusiastic about your goals? If not, do what it takes to make it so!

6. *Do exercises to help identify exciting goals.* One exercise to help you identify your goals is to make a list of things you are tolerating. This will help you find things about yourself and your life that you really want to change or improve.

   Another way is to work your way through your list of roles, making a list of twenty-five statements that begin with "Wouldn't it be fabulous if …" This is a brainstorming exercise—you are not committing to anything on this list while you are creating it. Afterwards, go through the list, make any changes, and decide if there are any items you want as goals. This is a really powerful way to explore new possibilities for yourself.

7. *Review and refine.* Goal setting isn't a five-minute job. It may take several sittings to finish it. If you do it well, it will be an enormous help; it can be a transformational process.

   When you feel that you have finished, leave it for a few days, and then go back over your creation. Most likely there will be things you can adjust.

8. *Take the final goal-setting steps.*

   - Make sure each goal has a completion date.
   - Identify the next step for each goal. Give that step a completion date too. It is very important to do this. People often want to rush on and start doing tasks once they know their goal.
   - Identify the next task(s) for the next step.
   - Schedule appointment times for starting the tasks.

- Keep working on your goals every week; working on them most days is ideal.

Managing Your Goals

How many times have you identified goals, perhaps even written them down, and then forgotten about them? We have all done this. It's the result of not having a system for managing them. This may well indicate that you also don't have a system for managing your life. If this has been you up till now, make sure you focus on chapter 16, "Systems That Work."

Being organized is not difficult, and the systems I have recommended will enable you to manage your life successfully. However, when it comes to goals that are complex, there are additional practices that will ensure their achievement.

1. *Plan the steps to the goal.* Although I discussed this in the section, "Setting Your Goals," I mention it again here because it is not a one-off activity. You need to keep working on identifying the stages or steps for your goals and projects, and the tasks in each step, all the way to their completion.

    The steps to the goal are the main areas of activity that need to be covered in order to achieve the goal. Let's take the example of starting an online business. Some important steps will include

    - deciding on the purpose(s) of the business;

    - deciding on the products: the range, source, cost, and inventory reserve;

    - deciding on the sales method(s) and locations: eBay, websites, etc.;

- finding storage and dispatching goods;

- developing the website, performing search engine optimization, and attracting traffic and sales;

- working through financial and legal issues; and

- securing other resources (e.g. staff).

The list of steps may not be perfect when you start. Fine—you can modify them whenever you get new information. Each step will have its own set of tasks. Write down as many as you can. Then, at least every week, and more often if appropriate, update your weekly tasks-for-completion list.

2. *Read, refine, and keep developing your goals.* Look for ways of extending the original goal. Make it a habit to extend yourself—to go way beyond what you would ordinarily do. Surprise yourself. Surprise those who (think they) know you. Having said that, take care in choosing the goals on which to extend yourself. You want amazing successes, not burnout.

3. *Visualize and experience the feeling.* The feeling I am referring to is that of having achieved a particular goal. Practise having that feeling every day. How does it feel to have that new car, to have that revitalized relationship, to have that financial or productivity achievement, or to have gone on that fabulous trip?

   Visualize what it looks like and feel the feelings of having achieved your goal before you choose the tasks to complete that day. Now, it's easy for me to recommend visualizing, but in practice this can be difficult, particularly if you are an auditory rather than a visual person. I found it difficult and put it off for years. I only start visualizing recently. Would you like to know what produced the breakthrough?

It came while I was practising recalling special memories. I suddenly realized that I could transfer the great feelings linked to past visual images into my future reality. I was able to get the visualizing process started with past images and feelings and then switch to visualizing and experiencing the feelings of having achieved my present goals. If the juices stop flowing, I go back briefly to my favourite memories again. I now start my visualizing sessions (before going to bed) by recalling special memories.

4. *Don't get stuck in the how.* You may remember that at the end of chapter 14, in relation to dreams, I said that it was important not to allow yourself to get stuck, wondering or worrying about how your dreams would happen. It's the same here in relation to goals. Your job is to identify the goals and the tasks. If you keep the goal alive as a really exciting prospect, seeing and especially feeling the feelings associated with having it, the hows will be answered in good time.

You need to be aware of the gaps—the places where you currently don't know how—but the key is not to focus on them as things that are missing, because that's a sure way to have them stay missing.

- Be excited about the goal succeeding.

- Be aware of the gaps—where a *how* is required.

- Expect the answers to show up, and they will.

Donna has proven this process dozens of times in her door business. One instance in which this happened was when she discovered bronze door skins that could be imported but found that there was no bronze paint available locally. The paint was essential so that the locally-produced door jams (frames) would be the same colour. No sooner had she put in her first order for the skins than Dulux put out a brochure with a brilliant new range of bronze paints. Problem solved. On another occasion she manifested the new car she wanted at the exact price she wanted to pay. Her manifesting skills are amazing.

One more time, don't get stuck in the hows. Focus on exactly what it is that you want.

5. *Be determined. Be persistent. Be regular.* Work frequently on your goals. Schedule thinking and planning time every week. This is when you work on your goals. Identify any bad habits you have had in the past in this regard. Choose new habits to replace them, and stick to them till they are part of your way of doing things without thinking or effort.

6. *Eliminate roadblocks.* The first point here is to keep identifying what you need, and then focus positively on it. When working on your goals, you will find that there are things that you need—specific needs. Instead of worrying about how you are going to get the needs met, affirm that what you need is coming to you. Be in action to have the need met, of course, but stay calm and confident in the goal's success, and use affirmations to maintain that positivity.

Here are some example affirmations that might relate to a new business:

- I am attracting the perfect website builder who will complete a great job in my price range.

- My new logo and website magnetically attract all who visit it.

- The income from my new business is fantastic, exceeding my budget and timeline.

The second road block to avoid is not planning ahead. You always need to be looking ahead to the next stage to be tackled, to the problems that must be resolved, and the next tasks to be done. Make notes; plan ahead.

7. *Document everything.* Documenting your progress through each stage and the plans for the next stage(s) may seem like a chore at first, but you will quickly be glad you have kept up with it. Life gets busy, distractions jump in front of you, and before you know it, you've lost track of what to do next to progress the goal.

But that's the old way. You *can* have distractions and then come right back to where you left off if you

- keep the steps to the goal up to date, and

- keep the tasks-for-completion list up to date.

If you have this information written down, you will always know precisely what stage you were working on and what to do next. The alternative is frustration and the wasting of time and energy. Distractions are inevitable, and you don't want to come back to work on your goal(s) only to find yourself adrift.

Summary

1. The most important question you can keep asking yourself is, "What do I most want?"

2. Your personal values are like your beliefs: they impact every area of your life. Keep track of them, and this will give you enormous insights and advantages. Your values will change over time.

3. Setting goals and managing them creates energy, brings experience, and enables you to manifest the life of your dreams.

4. Achieving complex goals definitely requires a system and the discipline to follow it. Written records and frequent attention to the process are keys to success.

5. Keeping your vision alive and keeping the steps and your task list up to date are similarly tremendously important.

6. Schedule the time for thinking, strategizing, and planning. Don't leave these to chance, because if you do, you will have taken your eye off the ball.

Practice

1. There are a multitude of things to do listed in this chapter. Please work your way through it and make a note of the tasks you plan to complete.

2. Visualizing.

   Because this is such a powerful tool, I want you to go back to that section of this chapter now and read it again. Then immediately spend thirty to sixty seconds visualizing the images and feeling the feelings of having brought one of your goals to fruition. You may need to use the special memories method to get started.

   Make this practice a regular habit. Please let me know about your results! Email me at adrian@SpinDoctor.com.

3. Create a vision board.

> There is one extra element that is really helpful in achieving your goals. That is a vision board: a board with photos or other images that show the main things that you want to manifest.
>
> You can find photos and text in magazines and paste them onto a board, creating an inspirational image of what you what to manifest in a particular goal or role. Alternatively, if you Google "vision board" you will find software and free photo sites that enable you to create electronic vision boards.
>
> A word of warning, though: plan the time you will spend creating vision boards. This can be very time-consuming. Don't let this enjoyable activity distract you from the goals themselves!

Reference

[1] Mapes, Richard. (2003). *Quantum Leap Thinking: An Owners Guide to the Mind.* Naperville, Illinois: Sourcebooks Inc.

PART IV

CREATING ALIGNMENT WITH YOUR DESIRES

CHAPTER 16
ACTIVATE YOUR MIND-BODY CONNECTION

> The rhythm of the body, the melody of the mind, and the harmony of the soul create the symphony of life.
> —B.K.S. Iyengar

One of the biggest barriers to creating what we want is the presence of conflict between areas of our minds or between the body and the mind. We talked about the conflict between our values, our fears and our desires in chapter 15. In this chapter, we are going to think about the alignment of our bodies and minds. There are several aspects to be considered here.

The Mind–Body Connection

There is a great deal of literature about the interaction between the mind and the body. All the evidence points to this being a two-way connection. The activity of the mind—our thoughts and feelings—has effects in the body. For example, people with depression are far more prone to general illness than those who are not depressed.

Body position and movement have measurable effects on the functions of the mind as well. Putting a smile on your face makes you feel lighter; your thoughts and feelings feel less intense. We have all seen athletes on sports teams with their hands on their hips, their heads and shoulders bowed, or their hands clasping the back of their heads. You know and they know that they are a beaten side. The All Blacks know the importance of body posture to their minds: standing erect with your chest out shows you mean business—you are not beaten yet!

We Give Priority to Mind Matters

In an earlier chapter, we talked about being present in the moment. When we are not present (i.e. when our attention is elsewhere) the body tends to be forgotten. For example, when I am concentrating on writing or sorting out a problem for one of my patients, I can forget to go to the toilet or to get a drink of water. Distractions can be dangerous when driving, when using a chainsaw up a tree, and in a host of other situations. Fortunately, I haven't had any toilet-related accidents as a result of concentrating on the things I work on.

Jokes aside, it is important to take note of the fact that our ability to register the information provided by our senses is seriously compromised when we concentrate on something that causes us to not be present. This is a sign that we are in the doing mode. When we give priority to the activity of the mind, we have given over responsibility for most things to our autopilot, and this can be costly.

Take Note of Bodily Sensations: They Are Signals

Changes occur in the body before we are consciously aware of them or of the emotional reactions that triggered them. For instance, changes occur in heart rate and the skin's electrical conductance before we are aware that we are starting to feel anxious, threatened, or stressed. We may get tense muscles in our necks, shoulder girdles, and backs after sitting at a computer for several hours. There is a need to balance lack of movement while seated with stretching every forty-five minutes or so. This not only helps our bodies, but it also gives the mind a break from concentrating. The mind, too, is helped by taking breaks.

In medicine, we find that people often present with symptoms late. Sometimes, this is because they truly were unaware of any until a critical change occurred in the function of one or more bodily systems. More commonly, the symptoms were ignored until, for example, someone told them to get their cough fixed or the discomfort was too severe to be ignored any longer. Putting up with something simple like a cough can result in hernias and impairment of bladder control. If unexplained weight loss and lack of appetite are ignored, the consequences may be more serious.

Important signals occur both with overwork and underwork, again advising us that something is amiss. Tiredness, feeling weak, and having difficulty concentrating can occur with both. The point I want to emphasize is that the sensations in our bodies provide us with a warning system. If we maintain awareness of this and (non-obsessively) practise monitoring our bodily sensations, we will learn how our bodies respond in various situations. We can then use that knowledge to detect when a change has started—an emotional disturbance for instance—and be in a position to take early and hopefully preventive measures (which are discussed in chapter 19).

We thus need to consciously balance "being in the mind" with "being present," for only with the latter can we be aware of what is happening in the body.

Breathing

Breathing is fundamentally important to human life. As the trademarked slogan of the Australian Lung Foundation states, "When you can't breathe … nothing else matters."

There are many sensations associated with breathing—the cooling flow of air through the nostrils and the throat and the sound that creates, the feeling of the chest and the abdomen expanding and relaxing, the sounds and sensations of clothing moving. All these are potentially direct links to being conscious of the body in real time. Focusing on the breath gives us immediate access to being present.

Awareness of the breath is thus one of the usual introductory parts of meditation because being present is a key part of meditation. Breath control is also very important. It is particularly important in scuba diving, in many sports, in playing many types of musical instruments, and in other physical activities.

In my specialty of respiratory medicine, I frequently see people who are referred because of breathlessness. Some have lung or heart disease, but many have no disease at all. They are breathless because the firing of their respiratory muscles is uncoordinated. They breathe with the upper chest while the upper abdomen moves paradoxically in the opposite direction. This results in hyperinflation of the chest, which makes the work of breathing much harder.

You can appreciate how this feels if you take half a breath in and then try breathing in from this higher set point. Because the work of breathing is harder, people breathe faster, blowing off carbon dioxide. The lowered level of carbon dioxide makes you feel very weird; you feel faint and light-headed, and sometimes you get a combination of numbness and a feeling of pins and needles in the face, hands, and feet. These are some of the main symptoms (or bodily sensations) associated with the so-called hyperventilation syndrome, which is more accurately called a disordered breathing pattern.

Our breathing is under the control of the subconscious mind, but as with other areas of subconscious functioning, the conscious mind is able to override the habit mind while intention is maintained. Thus, when a person develops a disordered breathing pattern, the solution to the problem is the conscious mind, which, through the repetition of exercises taught by a chest physiotherapist (or a respiratory therapist if you are in the USA), is able to correctly re-program subconscious control of the respiratory cycle.

Not only does how we breathe affect the sensations we feel in our body, but it also often affects the emotions. Breathing difficulty provokes varying degrees of anxiety, and people with severe hyperventilation syndrome are terrified that they are about to die when symptoms are at their worst. The good news is that this condition does not cause death. At worst, the person may become unconscious for a short time, but this is extremely rare. This clinical condition—which, as I said before, is not a disease—demonstrates the importance of being aware of our breathing, particularly when we are in difficult circumstances.

Let me give you a personal example of what happens when you don't do this. I'm pretty stable emotionally. However, I lost it in a huge department store in New York in 2013. My wife and I were due to fly to Hawaii late that afternoon. I left her in one of the three floors of women's clothing and went downstairs to the menswear department. Just one floor for that! After twenty minutes, I went back upstairs to find her. I couldn't find any of the landmarks I had taken note of when I went downstairs. Well, to cut a long story short, I went around all three floors of women's wear and couldn't find her. I did the same again, getting more and more anxious, with the same result. We didn't have our cell phones, and there was no public address system in the store.

Almost an hour later, Donna spotted me as I was walking past her. By then I was out of my mind with anxiety, short of breath, faint, and weak. I couldn't think straight. I had typical symptoms of hyperventilation. It was one of the most traumatic experiences I have had in recent times. I totally wasn't present. If I had been, I would have realized that she was sensible enough to go back to our hotel; we had to go there to collect our luggage before leaving for the airport.

If we focus on breathing calmly, at a normal rate and depth during highly charged circumstances, this will help us stay present and in control.

Look After Your Body

Your body is the golden goose of your life. Do your best to look after it, and it will continue to give you golden eggs. That is, if you look after your body, you are in a position to manage everything else.

How are you looking after your body? Can you improve your posture? What about your diet and what you drink? What else do you put into your body? Do you make sure you get enough sleep? Do you exercise regularly? Do you take the medication prescribed for you if you have conditions like hypertension, diabetes, and so on? Uncontrolled, these and other conditions silently cause permanent damage to many parts of the body.

A number of important aspects of "looking after the golden goose" are listed in the Practice section of chapter 5. If you have been avoiding putting golden goose care under the microscope, please check out that section again and spend a few minutes writing down what you could do better. Then decide what you are going to tackle first. Then prioritize and plan what to work on next.

Meditation

Meditation is practised by millions of people. Those who do not meditate are missing out! In essence, meditation involves the practice of regulating the mind. This may be done by contemplation of an actual object, such as a crystal or a picture; a meditation thought "object," such as love or compassion; a particular question; or an intent, such as opening oneself to the highest. A mantra can also be used. There is something you will become aware of when you reach a certain point in the meditation. It may arrive very early or come later during the course of meditating. It is an energy, one that may have the quality of an emotion, an aspiration, or a feeling of peace. When the energy linked to the object you are contemplating arrives, just hold that emotional energy and relax. Your conscious mind must still remain alert to your internal and external environments, but just allow your conscious mind step to one side as you hold the emotional experience.

The meditations mentioned so far could be called internally directed meditations. Externally directed meditations involve listening to music or to a guided meditation spoken by another person. A meditation suitable for beginners can be found in the Practice section of chapter 4. Meditation and mind chatter were discussed in chapter 11.

Maintaining awareness during meditation is important; in fact, meditation is a state of heightened awareness. Thus, although people who are meditating may look as though they are asleep because their bodies are still and their eyes are closed, their minds are relaxed, focused, and aware. In meditation, the aim is to remain lightly aware of the meditation object, any thoughts that arrive and sensations from within and around you, without thinking about them.

A practice common to all types of meditation is to notice when thoughts interrupt. Sometimes, the thoughts that arrive are valuable insights, and you may want to make a quick note with pen and paper. More often, thoughts are simply mind chatter about an unimportant or non-essential matter. In this case, the conscious mind's job is to bring you back to the present and to the meditation by focusing on the object, the breath, the sensations in the body, and the environment.

When the emotion or the special energy linked to the object arrives, hold on to that energy and to your awareness.

The result of this repeated, gentle exclusion of thoughts is that it trains the subconscious mind to become quiet for a time when instructed. It is in the space between the thoughts that most of the benefits of meditation occur. This is where personal consciousness connects with the universe.

The benefits of meditation are real. Meditation has a calming effect on emotions and helps with the development of insight and objectivity; mind control helps with emotional control. The health benefits of meditation have probably been best studied in relation to transcendental meditation (TM), and they are very impressive. TM is one meditation in which you follow a mantra. Meditation is practised by a wide variety of religions. Despite this, you do not need to be a spiritual type of person to do it, enjoy it, and benefit from it. Pleasure and contentment are benefits of meditation. There is also no doubt that those who are spiritually inclined are able to discover new depths of spirituality through meditation.

For further reading, I recommend a book by Graham Williams, PhD, *Life in Balance: The Lifeflow Guide to Meditation*[1].

Summary

1. Develop awareness of the sensations in your body. They are telling you something.

    - If something is amiss, look for imbalances in your activities and in your thoughts and feelings. What adjustments do you need to make?

- Use awareness of changes in the body as an early warning system of negative emotions so you can take preventive action, staying positive and present.

2. Many people's autopilot tendency is to give priority to matters of the mind, and thus to doing. Don't surrender to this habit. Remember to expand your attention—to your body; to your chosen, intentional way of being; and to the best use of your mind powers. We will be discussing the important topic of being and doing in chapter 18.

3. Consciously balance "being in the mind" with "being present," for only with the latter can you be aware of what is happening in your body.

4. Breathing is a wonderful gift.

    - It enables us to remain alive.

    - Focusing on the breath gives us immediate access to being present.

    - Focusing on breathing at a normal rate and depth during highly charged circumstances helps us stay in control.

5. Ignoring proper care of your body is a crime. Treat your body like a temple. Your body and your mind are your most valuable assets. If you look after your body, you are in a position to manage everything else. Make golden-goose care one of your highest priorities.

6. I highly recommend meditation.

Practice

1. Choose to adopt the following intentions: "My habit is to be positive. I generate positivity when it is absent. I smile. I am generous to others, and I am gentle with myself. If I cannot contribute positively, I keep silent."

2. Make notes about the sensations in your body, tracking them from when you wake to when you fall asleep. Do this occasionally.

    - How do you feel about those bodily sensations? Do they worry you, annoy you, or frustrate you? If they do, make a note to consider them again when you read chapter 20.

    - Do you need to do anything about any of these feelings?

3. If you are not exercising regularly, you are almost certainly not making full use or taking the best care of your breathing abilities. Consider doing some of the following:

    - Take six full, deep breaths, holding the breath momentarily at full inspiration. Doing this morning and night is a good practice.

    - Yoga exercise includes breath control. You might like to enrol in a course and challenge yourself.

    - Singing in a group is another activity that will improve breath control.

4. Review the Practice section in chapter 5. There are many suggestions there to help you take good care of the golden goose. This is the second time I have given you this opportunity.

5. I recommend that you give serious thought to taking on meditation as a regular daily practice. Start with five minutes per day. Increase the duration when it feels right. You might start with the technique described in the Practice section of chapter 4, or do some research online to find another technique that suits you. A detailed meditation on compassion is shown in chapter 21, although this may be too much at the start of your meditational practice.

Reference

[1] Williams, G. (2008). *Life in Balance: The Lifeflow Guide to Meditation*. Adelaide, South Australia: Lifeflow Publications.

CHAPTER 17

HONING THE POWER OF YOUR MIND

The empires of the future are the empires of the mind.
—Winston Churchill

At the end of chapter 16, I stated that our minds and our bodies are our most valuable assets. Let's look now at how we can sharpen and polish the powers of our minds. The topics in this chapter will enhance our creative abilities and make sure our habits of mind are aligned with manifesting exactly what we want.

Thoughts

In chapter 8 I wrote that a thought is just a thought, and thoughts can be changed. However, we also need to understand that thoughts have energy. It took energy to create them. That energy was imparted to them. Energy never disappears; it is always transformed into another form. In chapter 4, I talked about the dual nature of energy (such as electricity), which has both particulate (mass) and vibratory (energetic) properties. The energy of thoughts is the same as any other form of energy in this respect.

Because of their energy, thoughts have force, and as Mike Dooley said many times in his books, *Leveraging the Universe*[1] and *Infinite Possibilities*, "thoughts become things." This corresponds with a similar idea that what you think about, you become. These are huge reasons for us to monitor and manage our thoughts.

We don't have to allow our thoughts to hook us. It is important to be objective about them—to notice the content of our thoughts and not let them take their own automatic course. This takes practice, and for some people, it will be a major undertaking. Just remember, persistence guarantees success. Let's go further into this subject now, because we not only need to understand it—we must know how to manage our thoughts and practise managing them until it is a habit.

Thoughts fall into only two categories: helpful or harmful. Helpful thoughts keep you linked to happiness, gratitude, success and the present moment. Harmful thoughts do the opposite—they are associated with feeling unhappy, dissatisfied, and with what's wrong. This information is one of the most important keys to managing not just your thoughts, but your quality of life. As I have explained elsewhere, to be most successful in creating now, the conscious mind must lead. It must take on the task of staying present, observing your thoughts in real time, and deciding whether the thoughts that are running through your head are helpful or harmful.

If your conscious mind finds you are listening to harmful thoughts, it must recognize that your junior autopilot has been running the show, and take over from it. You consciously switch your thoughts to helpful, beneficial ones, thereby also gently re-directing your emotions to more positive feelings. Achieving this may require taking action, such as reading a few positive paragraphs, watching a short, empowering YouTube video, focusing on something beautiful near you, such as flowers, or recalling a happy memory. You do what it takes to get your thoughts back into helpful territory.

This epitomizes the training that is required to make your conscious mind the leader of your thoughts and feelings. In the last chapter, we talked about meditation and said that it is a state of heightened awareness. This is exactly the state in which we want our conscious mind to be during all our waking moments. Meditating helps train both the conscious and the subconscious parts of our mind.

Thinking

What most people call *thinking* is just having automatically-generated thoughts. True thinking involves using the analytical powers of self-consciousness, considering our options, and complementing these with the fresh possibilities generated by the imagination. Without imagination, we would just do the same old things over and over again, hoping for different results. This, of course, is the definition of insanity.

When you need to think about something important, be intentional about it. Get into the habit of making notes—written documentation is always better than doing it in your head.

Choose What You Allow Into Your Mind

The statement "I am the master and commander of my thought police" appeared in chapters 1 and 2. Whilst this definitely applies to monitoring your own thoughts, it also applies to thoughts that enter your consciousness in other ways.

Information and entertainment are important avenues through which positive and negative thoughts enter our consciousness. Images of violence and of people indulging in anger, hate, blame, and other types of dysfunctional behaviour do nothing to support our aspirations and our intentions to be the best and to enjoy happiness. The same is true of bad language and blasphemy. These are all energy forms created by minds that are connected to the primitive side of consciousness. We do well if we only allow into our minds language that is beautiful and thoughts that are positive and non-judgemental.

So-called news in newspapers, radio, and on TV is almost exclusively bad news that vibrates with harmful frequencies. Most media stories have no connection with our lives and can be ignored without any risk of missing something valuable. This type of news is, for the most part, an exact match to where many people's attention and thoughts are magnetically attracted—namely, to stories about what's wrong. Just check: are you a magnet for what's wrong? Is this where your thoughts and conversation drift? If so, this is an important item to identify and change. As a species, we need to create the demand for news about success and progress; news that promotes happiness, cooperation and striving; *not* more strife.

Music and art can be uplifting, or they can lower the vibratory frequencies that radiate from our minds. Stand guard at the entrance of your mind, and allow in only good companions. Speaking of companions, do the people with whom you associate resonate with the intentions of your heart and mind?

How much uplifting content are you sending or receiving in phone calls, text messages, and emails? If you find any rubbish—any at all—get rid of it. Don't read it or listen to it. Mind pollution in any form is unwelcome.

Use the Power of Transparency

Donna and I were flying in the United States one time. Nearby, a baby started screaming and kept screaming for what seemed like hours. It must have been a low-budget flight, because there were no movies or music to hide in. Donna got off the flight exhausted and complained about the screaming child. I, on the other hand, was unaffected. Why?

I carefully used the first practice listed in the Practice section of chapter 5: deliberately choose the thing(s) to which you give your attention and those you won't. Then give all your attention or none. I also combined it with another technique, which I call the "power of transparency." It is particularly useful in dealing with sounds and can be used, for instance, if you find yourself distracted in meditation by sounds in the environment.

Allow the sounds to pass right through you. Offer no mental resistance. I used to find the barking of a dog nearby a distraction until I started using these two methods. With a little practice, you will find the power of transparency easy to master.

No Worries!

No worries is a polite throw-away comment we give to others when we are not really present, not thinking about what we could say that would actually be a useful contribution to them.

But there is a far more important meaning of the heading of this section. I should have called it "No More Worries." What are worries? Where do they originate, and why do they occur? You know the answers to all three questions if you have read part 1 of this book. Worries are recurrent thoughts that originate in the subconscious part of our minds. They are the products of a junior autopilot that has taken charge. Why do they occur? Because you are not present!

We know that worries come from the subconscious part of our minds because they arrive uninvited. We don't consciously choose them, but we allow them free reign because this is our habit—that is, if you are a worrier (and you must be if you get worried and anxious about being late, about what people are thinking, or about not having enough time, money, or love, etc.). Most, but not all people on the planet are worriers to varying degrees.

We know that our junior autopilots must be involved when we are worrying, because we said in part 1 that they love to be in charge and they love the past and the future, where they anchor our attention by producing all sorts of fears.

So how do you get rid of worries? You do this by putting your conscious, logical mind in charge. The conscious mind can instantly recognize irrational, non-productive worrying thoughts, if you train it do so. It can ignore those thoughts and put its attention elsewhere; or stay on the subject, analyzing any issues and deciding what to do about them.

I have written many times "Don't tolerate negative thoughts." The management of worries is part this intolerance. So, reorient your mind right now. Commit to being a solution finder, not a worrier. Step into this solution-finding role as soon as you notice worries arriving. Then put the steps shown in the following table into action.

Managing Worry

- The first step is to *notice that you are worrying*. Take a few moments to watch your (subconscious) mind worrying away. Notice what a futile activity that is.

- Next, *identify the underlying issue* (e.g., being late, having unpaid bills, etc.).

- *Create solutions to possible consequences* of the issue. You can either choose to do that straight away or do it with integrity at another time. You might decide to do this step when the issue has moved from the future into your present reality.

You will need to practise this strategy. Become an expert in using it, because it will enable you to happily empty your mind when worries come calling.

Managing Your Memory

We touched on memory training in chapter 2, where I suggested that you investigate the many methods that are available. Perhaps start by looking on Google.

For most people, however, memory training isn't enough. An invaluable way to assist your memory is to have systems of recording and use them regularly. In short, use lists and checklists. They don't weaken your memory; they actually train it, because when you create a list, you bring the items into your conscious mind.

I have a list that incorporates my intentions for the week, the habits I'm establishing, my goals, tasks for each day, and more. Let me know if you need a copy. As consciousness is fluidic, we need structures that enable us to use it to our best advantage.

Checklists can be created by listing all the main components of an area you are managing. I strongly recommend creating them for your current work, your career, home and car maintenance, health and fitness matters, all financial matters, and so on. It might seem tedious, but using comprehensive checklists routinely prevents important items from being overlooked. Without them, we may not act on items for years. I thought one of my rental properties was insured and was asleep to the fact that no monthly invoices were arriving and no amounts were shown on my bank statements. Then a water heater burst on the top floor, and water poured through the building for two hours before the jammed water main could be turned off. At that time, I didn't have a checklist for my properties, and it turned out to be a costly oversight.

Create Supports for Your Intentions

Good intentions evaporate if we don't do things that anchor them in our consciousness. Using a calendar, making lists of important things like goals, tasks, and lessons learned, and other simple practices all help us attain the best use of our minds. There are many other things we can do to keep us on track. Consider doing some of the following:

- using images on your computer or cell phone screen that reflect what you want.

- using apps that put reminder messages on your computer screen or phone.

- making a vision board showing things that you want.

- meditating to clear your mind, to link with your aspirations, and to open yourself as a channel for the highest.

- listening to music that keeps you centred, happy, and inspired.

- recording affirmations and listening to them.

- reading books that help you stay on track. (A daily reading programme keeps you in the conversation of continuing improvement.)

- having a few positive paragraphs saved so you can quickly read them, or a few YouTube videos you can go to when you need help to switch from harmful thoughts to beneficial thoughts and feelings.

- wearing something special, such as a crystal or a cross—something that you can see and touch that immediately provides a link to you at your best or to your highest goal.

The more imaginative you are in ensuring you stay on track, the better the results that you will create.

Striving Or Forcing?

We have to make an effort when we want to get anything done, even if it's just getting out of bed. Our will power and effectiveness grow as we consistently make the effort needed to do things in a timely way, to keep our thoughts and feelings positive, and use disciplined systems to keep our activities and our minds organized.

How much effort is the right amount? Can we overdo it? Let's talk about forcing first. We tend to use the most force we can muster when we are dealing with lots of resistance. If a farmer wants to get his crop harvested before the weather turns, or an accountant has a huge backlog of work with tax time looming, for example, autopilot often takes over and these people work and work and work, regardless of the cost of abandoning themselves to the task. Forcing is definitely a function of being in the doing mode. Forcing always comes with a cost. It implies there is an element of desperation in the situation.

Striving, on the other hand, involves a conscious decision to be and do your best. It is a function of who you are being, not what you are focused on doing. When you are being a great parent, for example, this is a conscious decision, and when you are conscious of, or present in the situation, you always have objectivity that allows clarity in your decision-making.

Striving builds character. Forcing invites failure.

Identify and Manage Your Problems

Problems offer great opportunities to practise using the powers of the conscious and subconscious mind. Not many people have learned that the quickest way out of problems is to deal with them systematically. Allowing problems to cause suffering and slow you down is the old way. Make it a habit to step into action early. I have developed the following system to enable you to deal with problems efficiently and effectively.

Preparation before Starting to Sort Out Problems

1. Create the right frame of mind before you set about finding solutions to your problems. If you are seething with annoyance and your focus is anchored to the thoughts and feelings of upset, the first thing to do is to get rid of that anchor. You won't have the free attention you need to be creative and to allow new ideas to come into your mind.

2. Now, hear this! This problem is not the enemy. Open your mind to the possibility that this problem is an opportunity. It could be an opportunity

    - to learn something valuable that, if learned, would perhaps keep you from having this sort of problem again;

    - to contribute to others or for others to contribute to you; or

    - for personal growth: to help you develop patience or to understand others better, to help you become more open-hearted and open-minded, to practise allowing instead of resisting, or to practise not having to be right.

3. Don't solve important problems in your head. Use pen and paper or your computer.

4. Identify your intention: what do you want the outcome(s) of the solution(s) to be, in general terms? Maybe it will be something like

- all parties respect each other and are satisfied with the solutions, or

- harmony preserved and the greater good served.

Finding Solutions

1. Document the problem.

    "Please state the nature of the medical emergency." These were the words spoken by the virtual doctor on *Star Trek: Voyager* whenever his program was activated. What he was saying, in effect, was: "You've asked for my help. Don't give me your interpretation or diagnosis of the problem. Don't give me your emotional reaction to it. Just give me the facts." In addition, they encapsulate a very useful management tool: documenting the details of the problem(s) you are facing. When you remove interpretations (based on beliefs) and emotions you get more clarity on exactly what you are dealing with.

    - Write down the details of the problem. Refine the wording so you get it down exactly right.

    - Break the problem into its components.

        - There may be general things like not having enough time, not having enough money, not knowing how, not having anyone to help, and so on.

        - Then there will be specific difficulties, such as having personal conflict, engaging people in your solutions, or creating a plan, for example.

    - Create either a list or a mind map that show the parts of the problem.

2. Identify your role in the problem.

    Ask yourself if you have been part of the problem or part of the solution. In doing this, assume (because it is true) that there is no middle, neutral ground. Then decide whether or not you are willing to be part of the solution.

3. Brainstorm.

    For each aspect of the problem, brainstorm up to six solutions, even if they seem ridiculous. Give yourself two minutes on each aspect, and then go on to the next one. When you brainstorm rapidly like this, you allow your creativity free-reign, bypassing the more analytical function of your mind. You will use your analytical abilities soon, but not during this important creative stage of the process.

4. Select, prioritize, and schedule.

    Go through all the ideas you have written down, deleting those that are out of the question. Select the actions you will take, prioritize them, and schedule when you will do them.

5. Stay fresh and alert.

    Take breaks as required, making sure they are not just to avoid the problem-solving exercise!

If you get stuck.

If you hit a roadblock and can't move on, then do the following:

1. Persisting and engaging your imagination is your way out. You may need a short break to clear your head and your heart. Then go back to the section "Freeing Up your Imagination" in chapter 7 and implement one or more of the actions listed there.

2. Make sure all thoughts about blame have been obliterated.

3. Ensure that you are not emotionally anchored in upset. We will be discussing how to manage upsets in chapter 19. Use the techniques shown there. Clearing yourself of upset will allow you to focus objectively on problem-solving.

4. When you have done the steps shown above, *then* look outside yourself—decide where else you can look for solutions. You might use Google, or you might ask friends or work colleagues if they have anyone who can help. Don't indulge in the habit of avoiding the thinking steps shown above, however.

Problem-solving is a skill. The more you practise using this system, the more expert you will become in working through life's difficulties rapidly.

Generate More Energy and Drive

It is easy to identify people who have high energy and have tons of self-motivation. Take a moment and make a mental note of a few people you know who fit into this category. Compare them with others you know who are the opposite in this respect. Which group is achieving more; and which group is more interesting and fun to be around?

It is easy to justify the fact that you feel tired more often than you feel energized because of the circumstances of your health, the state of your body, how busy you are and so on. In order to progress in the direction of feeling more energetic and having more drive or enthusiasm for life, the first important step is to decide that is what you want. Now go beyond *want*; decide, this is what I *demand*! This is what I am now taking full responsibility for achieving.

If you decide to take the road to having continuously great inner energy and power, your journey will be personal, different from others'.

The basics, of course, are having life balance, eating and sleeping well, exercising and having many of the healthy habits I discuss in this book. After that, it gets more complicated, because quality of life is influenced by many factors, such as our attitude to ourselves and others to name just one. Many of these factors *are* dealt with in this book. However, if this is a topic that grabs your interest, and you want to go further into it, I can recommend a book which tackles it systematically and gives actions that will lead you towards greater energy, success and happiness. It is called, *The Charge: activating the 10 human drives that make you feel alive,* by Brendon Burchard[2].

Summary

1. Our thoughts do not define us. Our intentions do that.

    - To prevent thoughts from hooking and anchoring in the mud of negativity, it is useful to bring to mind that a thought is just a thought.

    - Thoughts lose their power over us if we stop giving them any significance.

    - However, thoughts are very important and need managing, because "thoughts become things."

2. True thinking is an active, analytical, and imaginative process. Simply having thoughts is not thinking.

3. Stay alert, and be selective about what you allow into your mind. There are many ways our minds can be influenced—by people, songs, TV, email, texts, and so on. Choose positive people and things that help you learn and that empower you. Choose only the best. Stay away from the rest.

4. Organize yourself. Be enthusiastic about using checklists. Be creative. Do what it takes to support your intentions and your memory.

5. Strive to be and do your best. Keep the big picture of your life accessible, and aim for balance. Striving should not stray into forcing and won't if you give priority to who you are being, rather than what you are doing.

6. Problems will always occur. They are important opportunities. Don't just muddle your way through them. Become expert in using the problem-solving method and the worry-management method shown in this chapter. Then, while other people suffer through their problems, you will rapidly solve yours and gain from the experience.

Practice

1. Pick a busy day and a more relaxed day. On each, carefully note the sources that are providing input into your mind. Particularly identify the positive and negative influencers. Some sources are mentioned above in the section, "Choose What You Allow into Your Mind."

    At the end of the day, make a note of the ones that really stand out as being positive or negative. If you do this regularly, you will be able to decide easily which sources to remove or, at the very least, to pay no attention.

2. Organize your lists:

    - Be sure to have a list of your goals.

    - Make a list of your main intentions in life—perhaps using your list of roles as a starting point.

- Make a list of your problems.

- List the things that you need.

What other things can you compile into a list? Others were mentioned in chapters 13 and 15.

Why am I making these recommendations? If you are unsure, reread the section "Managing Your Memory" in this chapter.

3. Go to the section "Create Supports for Your Intentions." Identify the things you will do to support your intentions.

4. When you have made a list of the problems you face, pick an important one and use the problem-solving techniques and the worry-management method in this chapter to find great solutions.

   Schedule the time to work your way through all your problems in the same way. Continue to schedule problem-solving time for yourself.

5. Take the opportunity to learn from your big problems.

   Document and save in your Problems Solved file:

   - The main components of the issue

   - The different spin you put on the matter—the different perspective, different context or different belief that you applied.

   - The actions you were able to take as a result of the new freedom you experienced from the "new spin."

> - Put down all the details of the glorious result you achieved. How did you *feel?*
>
> - What did you learn?

References

[1] Dooley, M. (2011). *Leveraging The Universe.* New York: Atria Paperback.

[2] Burchard, B. (2012). *The Charge: activating the 10 human drives that make you feel alive.* New York: Free Press.

CHAPTER 18

BE YOUR BEST

> The will to win, the desire to succeed, the urge to reach your full potential ... these are the keys that will unlock the door to personal excellence.
> —Confucius

We are nearing the end of this book, and it's time to shift gears. The last few chapters have dealt with improving several potential causes of less-than-optimal performance that result from automatic responses or reactions. Now we are shifting into top gear. What we want to do now is speed down the motorway of success, and taking on the practices recommended in this chapter will enable you to do exactly that. Fasten your seat belt, and let's go!

Trying

Note that the title of this chapter isn't "Try to Be Your Best." The reason *try* is omitted is because there is no such thing as trying. As a doctor, I have had hundreds of people over the years who have told me they are "trying" to stop smoking or have "tried" unsuccessfully to stop. The fact of the matter is this: there is smoking and there is not smoking. In the same way, there is eating responsibly, and there is overeating (or undereating); there is driving responsibly, and there is driving recklessly. We choose which of these we take on. What we call "trying" is choosing to, or choosing not to, and indulging in some stuff in our head about stress, it being too hard, or some other emotional fascination.

In life, we choose to be or do some things and choose not to be or do others. In making these choices, people often invoke *trying*. *Trying* by definition means that we are allowing for a greater than 50 per cent chance of failing to achieve what we are setting out to be or do.

Eliminate *trying* from your vocabulary and your life. When deciding whether or not to strive for a goal or a change, be aware of the worst-case-scenario consequences that could arise, and if you accept them, then make a clear choice—for example, smoking or not smoking ever again, taking a new job or staying in the same old job, having a holiday away or staying at home. Choose, and if you decide to go for a higher goal, give it 100 per cent of your attention.

Identifying the goal, your reason for wanting it and having a plan that enables you to take baby steps to success will send a positive message to subconsciousness; attention to these factors increases enormously the probability of success. Setting off without these and merely hoping for the best is a great way to attract failure.

The Difference Between Being and Doing

The second thing to note about the title of this chapter is that it is "*be* your best," not "*do* your best." This is such an important distinction that we need to sort it out once and for all. We need to start at the beginning.

We read earlier that switching from the aware, deliberate functioning of the conscious mind to the autopilot mode happens seamlessly—we simply do not notice when this occurs. Unfortunately, switching in the reverse direction takes effort, conscious effort. However, the more often we do it, the easier it gets to identify when it's important to take over from our autopilot. This is because as we "wake up" and take over consciously, we are training the autopilot to identify and make us aware of the types of situations for which the conscious mind wants to be at the helm.

As explained in chapter 2, one of the principle characteristics of the conscious mind is its ability to focus—to limit our attention in order to achieve a particular result. The corollary to this is that when the conscious mind is focused on a particular set of tasks, the subconscious mind is then in charge of almost every other aspect of our functioning. This means that when we are focused on doing, we are not focusing on being. This is true until you train yourself to focus on both. Even then, the main focus must be on who you are being.

Let me explain what I mean by *who you are being*. We could use another term instead—*your mindset*. Let's consider how having a being can result in better outcomes in difficult situations.

Imagine you are in charge of a group of people whose behaviour is erratic or unpredictable, and you need to be on your toes to keep the situation under control. You could be in the doing mode or in the being mode.

In the doing mode, your behaviour is more likely to be reactive. As time goes by, you may become stressed, anxious, and even angry. The hallmark of being reactive is the tendency to become a victim to the situation instead of being responsibly in charge of managing it and yourself.

In the being mode, you are in charge of yourself. For instance, you are being a great mum (or dad), being a great friend, or being a highly competent professional (of some sort). In the being mode, you are responsive—you consciously choose your responses to the changing circumstances. You manage yourself responsibly and purposefully as you carry out tasks.

So at the next meeting you are chairing (when you usually feel stressed) or when you are next in charge of some unruly children, you might choose as your being, "calm, collected, and competent"—something short and easily recalled.

When you are studying and there is the risk of getting bored and losing concentration, you might choose as your being "ace student, ace [*pianist, accountant, etc.; the pinnacle performer in your area of study*]."

When you are with people that you struggle with, pick a being that helps. For example, you might choose as your being "ease and enjoyment." Or you might decide to be Mr. Generosity, because in this mode it is easier to recognize others' efforts and compliment them for their contributions.

Whatever being you create, stand in or identify completely with it. Then choose the best thing to do to manage the situation you are facing. In a sense, you will be acting as if you have the very abilities that you need to handle the situation professionally and successfully. It takes courage to step up and strive like this. Be sure to acknowledge yourself for it. Also, take note of the benefits that result from being courageous.

Being Your Best Versus Being Your Usual

You might ask, "Why should I try to be better than I already am? I'm satisfied with the way things are right now."

My answer to this is that no one *has* to change, or *has* to do anything I have suggested in this book. Only do what you choose to be right for you. I'm going to talk about being your best because I know it is incredibly valuable to do so. In the end, though, the choice is yours. However, if you are heading in the direction of "no," you might ask yourself why. Be honest with yourself—find the answers that resonate in your heart. Does this topic remind you of something (perhaps religion) or someone to whom you have "antibodies" because of past experiences? Are you feeling overwhelmed, tired, or bored? Are you annoyed because you don't like being told what to do? What's behind the *no*?

Most people would say they are already striving for the best possible, that they always do their best. I'm not arguing with this, but I would ask that you read on and see if there are any areas in which you might be and do even better.

The benefits of striving for the best from yourself are immense. They grow exponentially over time. When you do this, you are activating the law of attraction. You are giving your best, and at the same time, you are also attracting the best back to yourself. Like attracts like.

People notice and are attracted to people who give their best. These are the people who get things done and who are highly successful in what they do. For example, I know which taxi company in Auckland has the most courteous drivers because I have noticed how their consideration for other drivers stands out from the other companies. Their cars also stand out because they are always clean. When you have made *being the best* your motto and your automatic way of being, the world is your oyster. Great opportunities appear. All this happens because of the principle that what you focus on expands, which is part of the law of attraction.

Areas in Which to Practise Being Your Best

So far, the examples have been about behavioural or personality-type ways of being. Let's start this section with a different area in which to practise being your best.

1. *Facial Expression*

    I'm sure you have noticed people who always look anxious, angry, or worried. Their appearance is a total giveaway of their usual ways of being. Research has shown that facial expression has an important biofeedback function that results in the release of neurotransmitters that perpetuate the mood reflected by the activity of particular facial muscles. Interestingly, studies suggest that Botox, by altering facial appearance can apparently help break the vicious cycle of negativity for some people.

2. *Your Clothing and General Appearance*

    The care (or lack of care) you take over every aspect of your appearance says something about who you are being. This includes your hair, skin, makeup, jewellery, clothes, and footwear. Let's not forget your teeth and bodily odour.

    I know, there are lots of people who are in rebellion against formality, tidiness, makeup, and so on. They are reacting against the values of their parents, their schooling, or something else. To them, freedom is ignoring societal norms; they would rather do anything than fit in. The way they look says exactly that. Their lives do too. If this is your choice, it's entirely valid. But if you want something better than your present circumstances, think carefully about what your appearance says about you.

3. *Your Driving*

    How do you drive? Carefully and considerately? Rushing, racing, and using adrenaline? Dominating—pushing in, cutting off others, and having little regard for the other road users as long as you get where you want ASAP?

    How you drive reflects who you are being.

4. *Your Attitude towards Other Races, Other Religions, or the Opposite Sex*

    Do you look down on people of other races or religions or members of the opposite sex? Come on—be truthful. Think about what you say about them in moments of stress or tiredness or when they annoy you.

    If you find negativity at times in these areas, make up your mind to eliminate it. It doesn't serve you. It doesn't serve anyone. Remember the law of attraction. Be, and attract back, the best that you can. Strive for this.

5. *Your Speech*

    We all know how powerful words are. It's not just the content but the way words are spoken that affects us. There are several things to consider in being the best in the area of speech:

    - Use correct grammar—don't contribute to the abuse of any language. Consider taking a night class if you don't understand the rules of grammar.

    - Don't swear. It's ugly, negative, and unworthy of you. It is the language of those who are asleep—on autopilot.

    - It is more powerful to say nothing than to say something negative. Our judgements are always made from our own limited perspectives—we never see the full picture. If we were to consider that there are unseen parallel universes with an endless amount of different outcomes to every situation, many of which are influenced by our speech and our being, we would realize that what we say is terribly influential. Use this idea as a paradigm or an analogy to guide you. Don't be distracted by whether it's true or not, because that isn't the point. The point is that words have effects beyond those that are visible to us. Words create reality. Words attract a particular type of future.

- When you use your ability to be the best, your power of speech has the potential to further the best, the beautiful, and the highest good in the world. The reality produced by this can grow and grow as you develop expertise in this practice.

There is more about speech in chapter 11, "Listening and Speaking."

6. *The People You Live or Work With*

The people who are in our lives are there for a reason. Our attitudes towards, and ways of being with the people we live with are really important. In many instances, the old saying "familiarity breeds contempt" says it all. If this is true for you, make up your mind now to improve your being with the people around you. When you do this, you will fail from time to time, particularly in the early stages. It doesn't matter. Get right back on the bike—don't let failure upset you for more than a few moments. Be inspired! Generate inspiration and courage; *be* love and compassion in action.

7. *Other Areas of Life*

Think about more areas of life where you can aim higher— where you can be the best. Here are some areas to work on when you are ready:

- your body

- finances

- family

- your neighbourhood
- your country
- nature
- spirituality

What's Your Very Best?

You can choose beings that are ideal for specific situations. However, it is very powerful to identify what you are like at your absolute best. You may be able to do this quickly and easily, or it may take time. However, the way to discover your very best is to ask yourself these questions:

- What is my highest aspiration; what would be the pinnacle of my life?
- What would I be like if I achieved that?
- What level of perfection and positivity would I need to achieve that?

Write down a statement that encapsulates these answers. Refine it over time. This is you at your very best. This is the highest expression of yourself. Make it a practice to connect with this highest aspect of yourself every morning, saying it aloud and really feeling it. This is a simple and highly transformational practice.

Create the Best in Every Situation

When you are well practised in being your best, you will automatically strive to create the best in every situation. However, until that time, it will probably be helpful to have another strategy available. Instead of focusing on yourself, focus on the situation, and strive to make it the best it can be.

You may be disappointed that you were not chosen for something or that you received no recognition or thanks for your contribution. Perhaps your long-awaited holiday has been ruined by the weather, by the loss of your luggage, or by illness. Perhaps your spouse or partner has let you down badly. Whatever has happened, strive to make now be the best it can be. Create the best in every situation.

The best what?

- the best, happiest, most productive office, ward, or sports team
- the best time exploring, eating out, shopping, or relaxing to great music on your (apparently, possibly, or not really) "ruined" holiday
- the best meal ever
- the best performance—one that people will remember with awe for years to come
- the best, most caring, and most connected family

How do you decide what is the best in a particular situation? Ask yourself the key question: "What do I most want?" Link that one to this question: "What is the very best I can do that will contribute the most?" To have any value, your contribution must be freely given. You are not contributing in order to make yourself or anyone else feel happier or better about themselves. This is crucial.

When you strive to create the best, set aside your automatic resistance to being the best; that way you are so much more likely to succeed. Resistance is implicit if you are annoyed, sad, resigned, or upset.

Liberate yourself from these feelings. Have the courage, the resilience, and the stamina to create the best from nothing for no reason. Make it a game. Challenge yourself to create the best, no matter how things seem.

Summary

1. You were born with limitless potential. Your handicaps, difficulties, and problems were and are a gift to enable you to focus and develop your abilities.

2. Being a champion doesn't mean you have to get your name in the newspapers and on TV, though if you do, this may increase your potential to inspire others.

3. Be a champion for the things you choose to stand for. Don't let those things be vague concepts. Write them down: "I am a champion for/of …"

    I remember when I first did this. I looked at what I had written next day and was surprised. I was almost in disbelief. It took several years of repeating those carefully worded beliefs almost every day before I really got it at the heart level. Now, decades later, they absolutely inspire me, and enable me to be the best that I can be.

4. Choose your being frequently, and live into your being(s).

5. Be in action, being the best that you can. Be a beacon of light so that you inspire yourself, and make that light available to inspire and attract others of like mind.

6. Be the best. Create the best. Do both freely, for no reason. This is not a formula to be used in order to succeed at work, make the most money, get that girl, or achieve anything else. This is your

gift to life. When freely given, the rewards will be unexpected, surprising, and life-changing.

7. Be determined: you make a powerful and positive difference. Your consciousness contributes continuously to the collective consciousness. Make your contributions count.

This road will have its ups and downs, but the further you go on it, the more rewarding, the more successful, and the happier you will be.

Practice

1. *Create a few inspiring "beings" for yourself.*

    - What do you love to do? How do you love to feel? Use these as inspiration for creating a number of beings for yourself. Use your list of roles also to stimulate ideas. I have given some examples of beings in this chapter in the section "The Difference between Being and Doing."

    - Take a few moments and write down a list of situations in which you tend to be reactive or where you sometimes fail.

    Choose at least one or two of these situations—preferably ones which will occur again soon—and decide who or what you could be that would have you more empowered. Write down two or three possible "beings" you could take on.

    Visualize yourself having taken on one of your chosen beings, working your way successfully through one of the situations in question. Do this visualization again as many times as you like before the situation recurs. When it does happen, notice how differently you feel and how people respond to you.

2. *Put a smile on your dial.* You could make this your standard practice. Smiling can be inappropriate, so smile often, *except* when the situation calls for something more appropriate. A smile is much more attractive and more engaging than a bored or miserable appearance.

Don't frown or scowl. Lighten up. Let the lightness of love and happiness radiate from your face. People seeing you will think, "That person looks happy," or "There's a successful person I'd like to know," or something similar. People will feel happier and smile back, silently appreciating you for your gift. What's more, *you* will feel happier, less stressed and you will carry those benefits into your relationships and interactions with others.

In case you haven't gotten it yet, let this sink in: your smile does more for you than any make-up, plastic surgery, or fine clothes. Please keep showing the world your beautiful smile! For more on this subject, read *The Smile Prescription* by Rich Castellano, M.D.[1] I also recommend that you check out his video now on https://www.ImageLift.com.

3. *Choose your being or attitude before you drive.* Focus on your being also during your journey. If you do, you will be surprised at the change in your driving experience. You may well find yourself feeling compassion for the people who cut you off, and eventually you will probably find that this rarely happens to you.

You might use "caring and considerate driver" as your being, for instance.

4. *Create a being or intention for each segment of the day.*

5. *Hold a thought or create a being that helps you stop judging people.* Pretend you don't know anything about people; this frees you up to reinvent them, to see them in a completely different way. Really, you *don't* know everything that caused them to be as they are. A being (also an affirmation) that might support you in situations where you tend to judge others might be "I am curious and caring." Or you could use another affirmation: "I look for the greatness in people."

6. *How about being passionate about people today?* You could link that being to the thought of accepting everyone today just as they are. This would remove any inclination to struggle with people you find difficult.

    - You can be yourself, knowing what you want and allowing others to be themselves.

    - If other people do or say things that would normally annoy you, stay calm and centred. Choose what to say. Don't just react. Bring grace and resilience—your best— to every situation.

    - This kind of intentionality and expectation of yourself directs your subconscious powers in a very positive way. If you persist with this way of being, your subconscious mind will accept this as an expectation that this will be your normal, automatic way of behaving.

7. *Choose a being that inspires you.* Do not choose a being that you think or hope will change someone else!

> 8. *Be, do, and have the best today.* Make whatever you choose in these categories enliven your day or make the day special for someone else. You could be daring and choose to do the best in many, or even every activity you do today. Then you would have many things that happen today be the best. Continue this practice, and notice what and how things change.

Reference

[1] Castellano, R. *The Smile Prescription*. (2016). New York: Morgan James Publishing.

CHAPTER 19

DON'T LET UPSETS HOLD YOU BACK

> My parents were disappointed I didn't finish
> college, and they were really upset when
> I went to Hollywood to become an actor.
> I was a big disappointment to them.
> —George Clooney

This and the next chapter deal with the behaviours that are probably the most frequent causes of the difficulties we experience in life. These behaviours overlap, both in their cause and their resolution. Despite this, they are not identical. Let's start with emotional upsets.

Upsets are an emotional reaction to one of three possible causes:

- An expectation was not met.

- An intention was not carried out.

- A communication remained unspoken.

Understanding which of these has activated your emotions allows you to identify what went wrong. If you document and examine your upsets, you may find one or two causes that are usually responsible.

This may give you a place to start the process of putting an end to upsets. Understanding ourselves is the first step towards progressing beyond our limitations.

The Concept of a "Pain Body"

Our spontaneous emotional reactions occur automatically; we don't consciously decide which emotion we are going to experience and then set that one in motion. Our emotions are products of the subconscious mind. In dealing with negative reactions, we should first ask, "Why did I react that way to that situation? Would everyone on the planet have reacted the same way? Obviously not, so why did *my* emotional system suddenly flood me with feelings of anger, sadness, and inability to stay in charge of my thinking and speaking like that?"

Eckhart Tolle, in *The Power of Now,* writes about us having a "pain body." Imagine it as being like an emotional equivalent of your physical body. It is an emotional "form" that has been created by painful experiences from your past. Or think of it as being a virtual twin, or something like the virtual doctor in *Star Trek: Voyager*. Our pain-body program is activated by an upsetting event. Something activates a trigger, and our emotionally labile twin appears automatically.

Like physical bodies, pain bodies come in all sorts of shapes and sizes. The triggers that activate them vary too. Some are supersensitive, while others need a major stimulus to get a reaction. Where's your set point? Perhaps you are supersensitive in one or two areas and relatively insensitive in others? How can you tell? How often do you burst into tears, yell angrily at another driver or someone you know, or feel resentment? Having any of these behaviours means you can look forward to greater happiness and satisfaction by learning from the things that activate your pain body. We'll discuss how in the section below, "Learning from Upsets."

Upsets Affect Others As Well As Us

The organs of our bodies are connected and work together at a subconscious level. We have previously discussed the idea that the consciousness of all people is interconnected and that this too occurs at a subconscious level—below our conscious awareness. We have also discussed the mass mind, or collective consciousness, to which the beliefs, thoughts, and emotions of everyone on the planet contribute. Through subconscious interconnectedness between people, it is possible for our individual pain bodies to be influenced by others.

Why mention this? Firstly, it explains why we sometimes become unexpectedly emotionally activated or more upset than usual. Also, it points to the responsibility we all have to project positive influences rather than negative ones in our thoughts, words, emotions, and deeds.

It is my personal view that one of our important tasks in life is to do what we can to heal the past emotional injuries that act as trigger points for further upsets, or in other words, to heal our pain bodies. If we work on this with commitment, our potential for being powerful centres of light and love, the quality of our service, and the quality of our lives will be increased enormously. Learning from our upsets is the obvious place to start, and we will discuss this in a moment.

Avoiding Creates Resistance

It is normal to resist having painful experiences. Unfortunately, resisting because we want to avoid an emotional trigger always carries a cost.

- First, the issue persists in your subconscious mind. That old saying is absolutely true: "What you resist persists."

An example of this is avoiding strong authority figures because of being sensitized earlier in life by a dysfunctional, dominating parent.

- Second, avoiding situations that may cause pain limits our spontaneity and freedom.

- Third, resistances in our systems require mental and emotional energy to maintain them. There is a school of thought that says that this diverting of energy has a negative impact on our immune systems and on our physical health. An example here is stress. Stress is caused by resisting situations and people we would much rather avoid. Chronic stress encourages vascular disease that causes heart attacks and strokes. Thus, it seems that negative energy from important emotional resistances is somehow subconsciously transferred into harmful changes in the body.

We will come back to the subject of resistance in the next chapter.

Managing Your Way Out of Upsets

Recognize Your Usual Automatic Thought Sequence

We can't stop having thoughts. The subconscious mind is an unruly chatter box: it is always having thoughts, and that won't change. When we get upset, we automatically do two things with thoughts:

- We judge ourselves and the other parties involved. We decide that we or they are either fabulous, fatally flawed, or somewhere between these extremes.

- We look for evidence that the judgements are correct. Only occasionally do we look to see if they are incorrect. Either way, we always look for evidence. We can usually find some sort of evidence that our judgements are correct—our junior autopilots love to be right—and this strongly encourages more thoughts in the same vein.

All the negative effects of thoughts are due to these two things. They create perfect conditions for a self-sustaining feedback loop where, by the law of attraction, negative thoughts attract more of the same. Our emotions are right behind. Before we know it, they have swept in, and a good old upset is in full swing.

However, thoughts lose their power over us if we stop giving them any significance. Let's look at how we can do this.

Get Your Impartial Observer to Interrupt

In chapter 3, we read that the conscious mind has the power to be an impartial observer, looking at the functioning of both itself and the subconscious mind. It is this ability that will enable us to control our thoughts and feelings.

Get into the habit of being your own impartial observer. When situations start heading in the direction of possible upset, intervene straight away by putting on your impartial observer hat. Like me, my wife, Donna, has practised doing this. We were discussing the practice, and she spontaneously made the observation, "It's like having another person there helping you."

Your impartial observer is perfectly capable of seeing one or more negative thoughts and feelings and advising you, "Hey, they're just thoughts and feelings. That's all they are!" Thoughts and feelings can only feed on themselves, create havoc in your mind, and create tension in your body if you ignore your impartial observer and go back to the old victim habit in which you allow thoughts and feelings to take over.

Note that this process does not involve suppressing your thoughts and feelings. It merely involves seeing them for what they are. When you recognize their insignificance by remembering that the thoughts you are having are just thoughts, you truly are present. Your conscious mind is in control. Now you are able to choose the actions that will give you the best results.

This sounds easy. It won't be, the first few times you do it. Do it consistently, and you will be amazed at how upsets either don't occur or become really brief. I've had to practise this innumerable times while writing this book. Believe me, this technique is gold!

Move to Higher Ground

An important principle whenever you are in the grip of negative emotions is to be intentional about moving through them efficiently, eliminating their effects, and moving on. Be aware, though, that powerful emotions cannot be switched on and off like light switches; it just doesn't work that way. Prevention is really helpful here, and this requires that you know what you want and stay present. This enables you to interrupt negative thoughts at the earliest possible moment.

If you can anticipate trouble ahead, activate your impartial observer and move your intentions to higher ground before trouble arrives. Let me give you an example to explain what I mean. Donna and I had major problems getting consent to build a barn for storage and an art studio at our home in the country, which is down a private road. We couldn't get our neighbours to sign an agreement technically required because the barn needed to be a couple of meters closer to the boundary fence than council regulations allowed. Ten months had passed, and we were still in the same position. We had to go to a roading meeting with all the neighbours. We moved our intentions to higher ground before we set out by deliberately going with the intention of having happy, neighbourly relations with them. The meeting went on for three hours, and we maintained our intention, even though there were some tense moments. The result was that everyone left the meeting as genuine friends—not as neighbours with an unresolved grudge.

Moving to higher ground means making the decision to be the best that you can be; and being committed to achieving the best outcome possible. You will remember that we discussed this in detail in the last chapter.

Learning from Upsets

Inner healing becomes possible when you make it your goal. Learning about your limitations and then striving to go beyond them is how to make progress. Here are three activities to get you started:

1. *Use the world as a mirror.* You may remember that I suggested this back in chapter 5 as a way to find out what your subconscious mind is telling you. Here we are using that mirror in a slightly different way. When someone says or does something that upsets us, the last thing we think to ask is whether or not we ever do the same sort of thing to others. However, this question does need to be asked. Leave it until most of the upset feeling is behind you and you have regained your objectivity. Then ask yourself if there is *anything* you have said or done that might cause a similar upset to another. How are you like that? Have you ever blamed someone without knowing all the facts? Have you ever become really angry and snapped back hurtfully? How have *you* acted without empathy or personal integrity?

   Maybe you won't find anything. But the more often you look and the more open and honest you are with yourself, the greater the chances are that you will find yourself having done something similar.

It is very sobering but also extremely powerful when we discover an aspect of our behaviour about which we were unaware. When we identify our own negative behaviour, our first response might be to feel ashamed. Well, that's our judgement habit leaping forward. Judgements are never helpful. What is helpful is to increase our awareness and resolve never to repeat that behaviour. Chances are, we *will* fail again sometime in the future, but this will be another opportunity to learn, to heighten our awareness again, and to renew our commitments to never failing again in that way.

Keep using the world as a mirror. Look out for it reflecting your greatness as well as showing you areas to improve. Above all, use it to develop your compassion and appreciation for yourself and others.

2. *Look for the costs and the pay-offs.* Reacting negatively to events isn't a powerful way to live. Negative reactions—such as anger, apathy, depression, and fear—suck the enjoyment right out of life. They poison us and the people around us. It's time to take full responsibility for eliminating them.

- Think back, and write down the events that happened last time you got upset.

- Ask yourself, "What did getting upset cost me?" For instance, take a look at what others thought of you or would think of you if they knew? How good of a role model were you for those around at the time, or for your children if they had been present, for instance? What opportunities were lost? Write down the answers.

- Now ask yourself, "What was the pay-off in indulging in the behaviour of upset?"

Did it help you get your way? Did you feel justified ("I was *right!*") afterwards?

Did you escape some responsibility? Look very closely here.

3. *Be committed to self-improvement.* Write down the things you decide that you will improve. What behaviour do you want to manifest? Patience, mindfulness, love, or will power? Review your list, making notes about your progress and your insights regularly—every day at first.

Putting an end to Upsets

People vary in the frequency and depth of the upsets they experience. Habit plays a big part in both. Learning about yourself, in terms of the causes—the three types discussed at the start of this chapter— and the situations and people that trigger them, gets you started in the process of putting an end to the way upsets can dominate life.

Learning to be more objective—looking at situations as an impartial observer, without becoming emotionally triggered—is an important skill that comes with practice. To help with this, remember that

- problems are always a gift because they are opportunities to learn and to improve, and

- we never see the whole picture; there are always opportunities in every situation, even when that seems impossible.

If you are prone to frequent or sudden upsets, I strongly recommend writing these points down; perhaps put them on a card that you will either carry in your wallet or put somewhere where you will see the list frequently. Another thing you could do is write down these two statements every day for at least a month; writing stuff out over and over was how I learned back in my school days. Whenever life stops going your way, get your card out and read it as many times as necessary to get these important messages into your conscious mind.

Emotional upsets are normal, when they occur occasionally, but you can make them a thing of the past.

Summary

1. There are three basic causes of emotional upsets: unmet expectations, thwarted intentions, and undelivered communications.

2. Upsets are opportunities to find our emotional triggers. These are the result of unhealed past emotional injuries. Until they have been healed, we will continue to react automatically with upsets whenever those past unresolved issues are activated by current events.

3. Wanting to avoid getting upset is understandable, but doing so allows the underlying emotional injuries to persist. Also, avoidance creates resistances in our minds and our bodies and thus affects our physical and emotional health. It is far better to address issues that have an emotional charge. When you resolve them, you will stop blaming and start forgiving yourself and others.

4. Get into the habit of activating yourself as an impartial observer as soon as situations start heading in the direction of upset. Identify your intentions, too—what you want as the outcome of the situation. Doing this allows your conscious mind to be in control.

5. I have given you a process for managing upsets. Write the key points on a card or have them available on your mobile device

so you have immediate access to them. Read them before going into situations where conflict might arise.

Practice

1. Read through this chapter and identify the things that you need or choose to do.

    Schedule the time to complete the tasks you discover.

2. Write out a plan for preventing and managing future upsets.

    - Read it regularly, so you know exactly what to do.

    - Keep a record of the outcomes—list both your successes and where you could do better.

CHAPTER 20

FREE YOURSELF FROM INNER RESISTANCES

> Resistance is futile.
> —The Borg, in *Star Trek*.

In chapter 18, we spent time looking at and thinking about being the best that we can be, and in the next chapter, we are going to take a more in-depth look at creating happiness and love for ourselves and others. Almost inevitably, there are things that can hold us back from both if we don't deal with them. They are the things we have been resisting.

What Is Resistance?

Resistance involves opposition. It is a principle that can be found in almost every aspect of life. In medicine, there is antibiotic resistance—the loss of susceptibility of microbial organisms to particular antibiotics. In my own specialty there is airway resistance, which impacts the ease with which air flows through the larynx, the large and then small airways, to the alveoli, or air sacs, where gas exchange occurs. Airway resistance is increased in asthma and chronic obstructive pulmonary disease, making breathing difficult because more effort is needed to move gases into and out of the lungs. Sudden increases in airway resistance can be life threatening. When objects from space descend in free fall through the earth's atmosphere, air particles provide resistance to their passage such that they heat up to incredibly high temperatures. Resistance to the flow of electrons (electricity) similarly generates heat.

Resistance is thus an important property in physics, but it is also seen in various aspects of human consciousness and behaviour. We talk of resistance in military and political contexts and in psychology. When someone has a point of view that is very different from our own, we may resist accepting that theirs may be valid or correct. The more attached we are to our points of view, the more we resist theirs. Wars and other types of conflict often start because resistance generates heated emotion.

Being Right

Wanting, needing, or having to be right is a perfect example of inner resistance. It is a giant trap that currently affects much of humanity and prevents people's inner beauty from shining through. Having to be right is a classic example of our junior autopilots actively at work in the personality, resisting threats to their importance. In chapter 3, we learned that this more immature, habitual part of us strongly holds the belief that it is all-important (to itself). It badly wants to stay in control and will do almost anything to maintain its survival. Our junior autopilots reside outside of our awareness in the subconscious mind.

If we are to be actively creating now, the conscious mind must stay in charge. Subconsciousness is the servant of self-consciousness, but we all allow subconsciousness to run things at times. The trick is to know when to allow subconsciousness to be at the helm and when to command it to step aside.

The need to be right can quietly slip into relationships where there is already conflict. For example, teenage daughter is rude and lazy. Mum is annoyed about this: she can't help but tell daughter what to do (because doing those things will work; they are the "right" things to do). If Mum would stop being right, make sure the rules are understood, and allow the daughter to choose her own way, the conflict in their relationship would disappear. They would stop resisting each other. Although this is an oversimplification in the interests of space, I hope you see the principle I am suggesting.

We can make a conscious choice not to put up with a demanding, self-important junior autopilot running our behaviour. When we make that choice and consistently keep making it, we tell the subconscious mind that this is the norm. Until we have trained ourselves in this new way of being, the less developed, automatic part of ourselves remains the source of our resistances.

Identifying What We Resist

It's not hard to spot when we are resisting something or someone. It's happening when we feel an inflamed emotion—in other words, when we are feeling negative in some way. Often, the emotion will start with a feeling of annoyance. This may grow—if we allow it— into outright anger or even white-hot rage.

How our inner emotions translate into speech and action varies. We may overtly show our feelings in certain circumstances, but often, we slip into habitual patterns in an attempt to disguise them. For example, we sometimes hide the extent of our upset by giving the other person a look and make a slightly cutting remark. Another habit is avoiding certain people, as mentioned in the previous chapter. When we have been resisting for a long time, the emotional signal may be much less obvious because we have become well practised in suppressing it. This is likely to make the underlying cause harder to find.

The thing about psychological resistance or resistances in consciousness is that there is always a cost. When we considered the comfort zone in chapter 10, we saw that there was always a benefit and a cost. Staying in the comfort zone is a great example of resisting. Another situation when we automatically resist something is when we are conflicted—that is, we having conflicting desires. At these times there will almost always be an accompanying negative emotion.

Negative emotions themselves are not bad. We may be able to shake them off quickly sometimes, but often, people get stuck. Then the negative emotions get in the way. When this happens, our attention gets hooked and anchored, as we discussed in chapter 5. Until we get free, we are stuck in an automatic cycle of thoughts and feelings that sucks away our energy, our effectiveness, and our happiness. How can we get free?

Move to Higher Ground

It is almost impossible to resolve big upsets and to tackle the issues behind them if you have sunk into the quicksand of anger, resignation, and other powerful negative emotions. You need to use some pretty strong equipment to pull yourself out. Most people don't have that equipment available.

For many people, slipping down into negative emotional feelings has been the habit of a lifetime. If this is true for you, you will need to give priority to creating the new habit of moving immediately to emotionally higher ground as soon as difficulties appear. Happily, you will quickly be rewarded for your success.

The rest of this section will give you the equipment that will enable you to get yourself out of the emotional mire. The first thing you need is at least neutral or free attention. Neutral attention means you are free of emotionally charged thoughts and feelings; you are nowhere near either extreme of the emotional scale; your attention is not distracted by your emotional state. Even better than neutral would be the feeling of positive motivation.

Next there are several steps. The sequence is important, so don't leave any out.

1. *Identify the thought(s) that are causing the problem.* When you are feeling down or even lower on the scale of emotions, it's because something happened and you had a negative thought or maybe several negative thoughts about yourself. Identify those negative thoughts, and you are halfway towards escaping that quicksand.

    So what was that negative thought? Could it have been something like one of the following:

    - *I'm not good enough;*

    - *He/she is so horrible to me;*

    - *I hate it when that happens, and it always happens to me;*

    - *I'm so frustrated and angry!*

    - *This is so unfair!*

    - *Okay, I'll do it, but I really wish I was doing something else.*

    - *I can't …*

    - *I haven't got enough [time, money, etc.] to do that.*

    - *I just don't know how to …*

    - *This shouldn't be like that!*

The last statement in the list above is probably the one that fits most causes of negative emotions. However, if none of those listed really fits your situation, look hard and create the statement that does.

2. *Interrupt the negative thought and replace it with a happy thought.* You will remember that this action was recommended in chapter 1 and, in more detail, in chapter 6. In this step, you recognize that the negative thought that seemed so significant was just a thought. Let it go. "Good-bye, old thought." Straight away you feel happier.

   This is an important step in getting to higher ground. Please don't omit it.

3. *Recognize that thoughts do not define who you are.* Because we constantly have thoughts, people tend to identify with their flow of thoughts and believe that this is who they are. However, this simply isn't true. Your conscious mind can interrupt the flow of automatic thoughts and replace them with something completely unrelated. Your conscious mind can put you back in control. You can choose the real you.

4. *Choose the real you.* Maybe you have (habitually) thought it was natural to put yourself first before everyone else. Or maybe you have always thought the exact opposite. Who you are is what you choose, and you can do this either unconsciously or consciously. You have the power to deliberately choose now and to choose again whenever you want. You were always able to do this, but maybe you got stuck allowing your habit mind to choose for you. This is quite usual. For most people, who they are being is purely an automatic reaction to something—the weather, how they feel, what someone said, and so on; the list of possibilities is endless.

   Choose who and what you are and will be in every moment. Don't let your habit mind choose for you!

5. *Connect with your highest.* This is how you step up to higher ground. We discussed this in the context of being your very best at the end of chapter 18. In brief, I said there that to connect with your highest, you ask yourself three questions:

    - What is your highest aspiration? What would be the pinnacle of your life?

    - What would you be like if you achieved that?

    - What level of perfection and positivity would you need to achieve it?

    Be sure to do this exercise and to create a sentence or two that describes you at your best. Make sure this statement is easily available on your computer and cell phone. Reading and emotionally connecting with this synopsis of you at your best is such a powerful thing to keep on doing.

    When you really connect with your highest, this instantly becomes who you are. Your heart sings, your mind becomes clear, and you have freedom to choose the best way forward without the demands of your less developed, autopilot self. You might decide to tackle the issue that caused your upset immediately, or not. You have freedom to choose. You might decide you need a break, more information, or just a good night's sleep. Perhaps brainstorming is the next step. Now you have free attention, you can plan the strategy that will resolve the issue behind the upset. You are ready to move past the previous resistance.

Moving Past the Resistance

If you have taken that higher ground, you are ready to move on past the previous resistance. This isn't difficult; there are only four questions to answer. I can't believe this is so easy and so obvious, once you know how.

The important preliminary step is to identify the issue you are dealing with. Make sure you phrase it in neutral or unemotional terms.

- The first question to ask yourself is "What do I most want here?"

- The second is "What is/are the thought(s) that will give me the feeling of having what I want?"

- The third question is "What have I been resisting?"

- The final question is "Setting aside that resistance, what am I going to do to have what I want?"

Let's look at some examples:

1. "I don't like (the physical aspects of) my home."

    Q: "What do I most want here?"

    A: "I want my home to look more inviting."

    Q: "What is/are the thought(s) that will give me the feeling of having what I want?"

    A: "I love my home. I care for everything in my home."

    Q: "What have I been resisting?"

    A: "Doing the things that someone would do who really cared for their home."

    Q: "Setting aside that resistance, what am I going to do to have what I want?"

A: "I am going to make my bedroom and the kitchen impeccable today. I will have the whole house looking gorgeous, including getting the windows cleaned and the place repainted by [insert deadline]."

2. "I don't like my boss."

    Q: "What do I most want here?"

    A: "I want to feel good about working at my work place."

    Q: "What is/are the thought(s) that will give me the feeling of having what I want?"

    A: "I am a star at work. I make a difference there."

    Q: "What have I been resisting?"

    A: "Being creative in making a difference at work."

    Q: "Setting aside that resistance, what am I going to do to have what I want?"

    A: "I am going to be happy at work and make being happy part of the culture there. I am going to be a champion for the idea of people helping people there."

3. "I'm fed up with not having enough money."

    Q: "What do I most want here?"

    A: "I want to enjoy fabulous surroundings and a great lifestyle."

    Q: "What is/are the thought(s) that will give me the feeling of having what I want?"

A: "I have everything that I need. I love being generous to others."

Q: "What have I been resisting?"

A: "Doing something about the feeling of being not worthy of riches and happiness. Doing the planning and taking the actions I need to do to get what I want."

Q: "Setting aside that resistance, what am I going to do to have what I want?"

A: "I am going to eliminate those old negative thoughts and allow riches to flow into my life. I am going to be grateful for what I do have and share my riches and happiness with others. I am going to set goals, act on them, and attract the surroundings and lifestyle that I want."

Let's summarise the four absolutely essential components of the process of moving from resistance to solutions in the following table.

Moving from Resisting to Finding Solutions

1. Stand powerfully for being your best.

2. Identify the specific issue, and the type of outcome you want. Make this something that is achievable.

3. Take responsibility for managing the situation and the outcome that you want.

4. Be willing to put the demands of your junior autopilot aside—particularly that of being right. If the person in example two had been stuck in being right about his boss being the problem, finding a creative, positive solution would have been almost impossible.

Purposefully tackling the things we resist and having a method for doing this really works. This process for moving to higher ground and then moving past resistances is not for the faint-hearted. You may find it easier if you are able to get a partner—someone you respect and trust—to work with. Definitely be patient with yourself. Be committed to success. Don't give up. Failures are not failures—they are merely opportunities to keep going and to get stronger. You wouldn't give up if you were tired and exhausted after workouts in your first few weeks at a gym. Treat managing upsets and issues the same way. Take a break when you need to. Then get going again. Just keep using the process; keep training your will-power muscles.

Purpose

The Purpose of People and Events

Every person and every event in your life has a purpose.

Think about that statement. Memorize it. It holds the key to transforming your life, if you apply it regularly. Let's take a look at why that first statement is so important.

When you consider your parents, your family, your friends, and all the people you know, the qualities you recognize in them are a reflection of those same qualities in yourself. Now, don't get excited about that last statement; please read on.

On the positive side, you can and should acknowledge yourself for the greatness, the generosity, the love, the commitment, and all the other positive qualities that you share with them. In frequently being aware of the positive qualities that we are expressing, we are amplifying their power in the subconscious and conscious parts of our mind. We are developing the best in ourselves. It is very important to do this. Identify your purpose in doing so, and this knowledge will strengthen your resolve.

On the negative side, there will be things that you dislike or even despise in some of these people, and you may want to say hotly to me, "You're wrong! I could never be like them!" I believe you. Of these negative qualities I should have written "they are a reflection of either the potential or the past potential for you to express those same qualities." Hopefully the latter is the truth, but we all have junior autopilots who are the source of our negative thoughts, emotions, and behaviours. Almost every individual on the planet has "Junior habits" to work on.

One purpose of seeing the negative qualities in others is to recognize that we have previously expressed similar negativity ourselves, perhaps in some other way. This will enable us to be grateful that we have learned that lesson and no longer need to think, feel, or act in that way. However, take a closer look and see if there is still a remnant of that behaviour in you, just because you can.

Learning to be grateful for what we have, where we have come from, and the lessons we have learned is one of the important purposes for the presence of people with negative qualities in our lives. But there is at least one more.

How do you feel about those people and their negative qualities? Do you dislike them? What emotion do they arouse in you? Perhaps some of these people have passed on or moved out of your life, but memories with some emotional charge still remain. My father died about twenty years ago, and for most of that time I was holding onto negative thoughts and emotions in relation to him. One thing I blamed him for was being an angry piano teacher who shouted at me and hit me at times during our lessons. At the age of thirteen, I could take no more and gave up on learning to play the piano. It was something I loved. What purpose could his behaviour and my reaction to it have had?

Within me was a great resistance to him. I was incomplete. Donna, my wife, recognized this, because every time I mentioned my father (which was rarely), she felt that emotional charge in my words and body language. I have done a lot of work over the years to resolve this, but the thoughts and emotion remained. It was only when I started looking at the purpose of that part of my life that I was able to become free. I think everybody has parts of their lives that they would rather not have had to experience. The piano episode was one of mine. But it had several purposes, and I'm going to list a few for you.

- It gave me a love of music and of piano music in particular. What a wonderful contribution to my life.

- I now have the opportunity to buy my own piano and start learning again, enhancing the neuroplasticity of my brain for the future. This will be a huge contribution to the second half of my life!

- I survived those hard times. I know I can make it through even harder times, if they come up in the future.

- My father's behaviour had nothing to do with me personally; his junior autopilot was running him, and I suspect he may have hated that part of himself. He was a perfectionist who could never achieve perfection. Looking back, I can see that those experiences helped me to learn how to look at people differently, to have compassion, and to be generous when the immature parts of people take charge. I don't know if my father ever really understood or forgave himself for his hurtful behaviours. I am so grateful that I not only understand them but have also learned from them this lesson of forgiveness.

- In writing this, I found another purpose for those past events in my life: to be an example to you. I hope my example of being set free by finding empowering purposes helps you to find, examine, and become complete if you have life experiences that still have a negative emotional charge.

This is an important topic, and perhaps there is a lot here for you to reflect on, and maybe read again. Please come back and reread this and do the Practice section of this chapter.

The Purpose of Your Life.

Another aspect of purpose is the purpose of your life. Way back in chapter 1 I said life has no particular, set meaning. It has no particular purpose. It's only meaning or purpose is what you and I choose and then say it is. Most people have not defined a purpose for their life. This requires thinking, and Junior wants you to have thoughts, but not to actually *think*. Finding your life's purpose may take time. The places to look are in the things you love most—in your job, your hobbies, your interests and activities, your family, your neighbourhood, your country, and the world. To what might you, or do you, aspire in all these areas, and why? What lies behind these aspirations?

If you have not identified the main purpose that unifies each aspect of your life, make it a project. Do some reading, talk to others, keep investigating, and then continue to refine it. At least find a high purpose for the things you spend most of your time and money on.

Remember that there is no one true-for-all-time, cast-in-stone purpose for your life. You *choose* it. It will be your true purpose, but allow for the possibility that it is your purpose only for the time being, that you may discover a newer, deeper layer. Finding your purpose is often a voyage of discovery, an ongoing enquiry. Enjoy it; don't restrict it.

Lastly, what is the purpose of your purpose? I would say your purpose is invaluable for the following reasons:

- It is a powerful link between your desires, your intentions, and your actions. It provides motivation. Whenever you notice the experience of resistance, even retrospectively, bring your life purpose to mind, and it will help you move past and resolve your resistances.

- It makes you feel more complete, because you have created an important part of yourself. You have brought new meaning to your life.

- It affords you the opportunity to grow into your purpose, which has added a new perspective to your life and thus opened up other new opportunities. Most likely these will be opportunities to give even more valuable service.

Give thought to this section and create your own list of purposes of your purpose.

To help you create your own purpose, let me give you mine, as an example. I have had a life purpose for many years, but I recently changed it to make it more practical. It goes like this:

My purpose is to be a radiant centre of Light and Love – a transparent channel for the Highest.

I energize every moment with joyful enthusiasm,

That I may inspire others to ever greater heights of awareness, productivity and generosity.

Practise Feeling Completely Free of Resistances

It makes sense that the fewer the number of resistance circuits there are in the subconscious mind, the less stressed, the happier, and the more creative you will be. Use the four-step method above to clear specific resistances as soon as you can after you find them.

In addition, it is worth practising being an open channel, free of all resistance. You can do this for a few minutes when you wake up in the morning. Simply place your attention on the warm, comfortable sensations of your body and on being open, happy, and relaxed. Take this feeling with you, and return to it frequently during the day.

Doing this in the middle of the night when you wake up may be the thing that will enable you to go back to sleep quickly. Do not give any attention whatever to any concerns, problems, or things to do that arrive in your mind. Just return immediately to feeling warm and comfortable, noticing the motion of your breathing, and to your intention to be an open, happy channel—perhaps a channel for love and blessings. Melt into that love; allow it to envelop you totally. This is another valuable way of using the mind–body connection, which we discussed in chapter 16.

I suspect that the reason new ideas emerge while you are taking a shower is that, with your attention on the comfort of the experience, your creativity is able to flow. Now, you can't spend all your time in bed or under the shower, but these observations tell us something useful. If we can set aside worry and other negative thoughts and feelings and focus instead on our bodies being at ease and feeling happy, relaxed, and carefree, we will be able to be more creative. Hey, this is the circuit of success where I want to be, don't you? The first step: identify that what you want is to be happy, relaxed, carefree, and resistance free. What you focus on expands!

Summary

1. Resisting is an automatic reaction that consumes our energy. We know we are resisting when we feel the need to avoid and when we experience one of the obvious negative emotions. The feeling

of missing something or someone, that we don't have enough money, or that we are unloved—these are some of the many feelings of inner resistance. Self-righteousness—the feeling of being "right"—is another. Others are discussed in this chapter.

2. I won't repeat here the process for moving to higher quality emotional ground as part of moving past resistances. There are several steps, and you will need to study them in order to take it all on board.

3. Developing the ability to move your thoughts and feelings to higher ground is especially important. If you practise this every day, it will help enormously. This is one of the most important lessons in this book.

4. Everything has a purpose. Finding the purpose of emotionally charged parts of your life will enable you to set free the emotional energy trapped there. Creating your life's purpose and keeping it in mind will minimize resistances holding you back. Purpose is everything, so keep creating it!

5. Practise being an open, transparent channel, free of all resistance. Do this every day, too. This is another of the most important lessons in this book.

Practice

1. What and who do you resist?

    - Make a list of things that you resist at home.

    - Make a list of things that you resist in relation to your body and your lifestyle.

- Make a list of things that you resist in relation to the people (present and past) in your life.

2. Please re-read section five of "Move to Higher Ground," *"Connect with your highest,"* where I ask you to write one or two sentences that describe the highest expression of yourself. Practise connecting with your highest every day. Do this morning and night. If you do one exercise in this book, this is the one I recommend most.

3. Use the four-step method shown in this chapter for dissolving the resistances you have identified, one by one. In each case, make sure you come up with a list of actions you will take and dates by which you will take them.

   You don't have to do all this at one sitting. It would be impossible. There are probably weeks or months of work involved. The thing to do now is to set some time aside—schedule a time when you will spend, say, forty-five minutes getting started. Then schedule another time soon after that. You know, if you made up your mind, you could work on this project for thirty to forty-five minutes every day. Believe me, you would—no, you *will*—absolutely love the results. I would love to hear about them. Please let me know if you need help (email: adrian@spindoctor.com).

4. Find positive purposes for the experiences that cause you pain. Like me, you may have to work on this over time and when the time is right. An important purpose of those times might be to heal yourself by releasing the trapped energy there, but as I found, there were multiple positive purposes, some of which I created out of thin air. When you are ready, schedule the time to do this.

5. Practise the feeling of being free of all resistances—an open channel through which happiness and love are flowing into your heart and mind. Allow it to flow out through you to all others. Right now is a great time to start.

CHAPTER 21

LASTING HAPPINESS AND LOVE

> Life is not about finding yourself.
> Life is about creating yourself.
> —George Bernard Shaw

Before we get down to the new layer of gold contained in this chapter, I want to start by digging into some important surface layers, briefly revisiting two parts of the ground we have already covered.

Don't Tolerate Your Unhelpful Emotions and Behaviours

Happiness and love will never be a consistent part of who you are if you do nothing to improve the negative side of your emotions and behaviours. Because this is so important, we should look again at preventing negativity from sabotaging your aspirations. Managing habitual negative emotions and behaviours doesn't have to be hard. The following is a useful summary.

Managing Unhelpful Emotional Patterns

- To start, you must choose and make a clear intention to *be* happiness and love.

- Choose and write down the name of this happiness and love goal.

- Then write a description of what the new you, your new circumstances, and your whole life look like, having achieved this wonderful goal.

- Read it every day! Refine it and expand it. Make it great!

- Next, make rules that absolutely do not allow you to indulge in those old, unhelpful emotions and behaviours. Make a list of these emotions and behaviours, so you know what you are managing.

- Use your imagination to create and practise scenarios in which you have previously lost it. Insert your new responses, based on happiness and love. Keep your responses simple. Practise several times before you next get into that situation. Practise with a friend, if that is appropriate.

- Keep a list of your successes as the new you grows more powerful with time and practice.

- Don't allow any failures to move you off course.

This is only a brief summary of some of the important practices for dealing with unhelpful habits in our consciousness. If they are strong in your consciousness, it is very important that you go back to and engage fully with the material in chapters 19 and 20. Your first task is to interrupt your own habitual cycle of things like anger, upset, frustration, worry, overload, procrastination, the sense of not being able to stay happy and contented, or any other unhelpful behaviours (such as losing interest and intentionality) that you have automatically allowed in the past.

What Brings You Happiness and Love?

Love and happiness are often considered to be feelings or emotions. We all know what it feels like to be really happy. We say that we "love" our new cars, our hairstyles, feeling fit, and so on. However, when love and happiness are based on external factors, on particular circumstances, they are doomed to be transient, because they are reactions to those circumstances, people, or things. We have not consciously generated the happiness, so its source is the reactive, subconscious mind. Yes, it's great when we have attracted circumstances that really please us and everything is working out well, but what about when things aren't so good?

Moving Closer to Consistent Happiness and Love

Firstly, as just mentioned, it's important not to allow unhelpful emotions and behaviours to express themselves when things "go wrong." Actually, they haven't gone wrong; you have just been presented with a new opportunity!

Secondly, throughout this book, we have talked about things you can do to keep on track so that you continue to create the experiences and outcomes that you really want. We could call these the Seven Steps to Happiness and Love, which I have listed in the following table.

Seven Steps to Happiness and Love

- Don't tolerate negative thoughts.

- *Frequently ask, "What do I most want?"* This is always the key question, whatever the circumstances.

- *Keep focusing on your highest priority items.* Keep a list of your key goals, their next steps, the people you want to contact, and especially your dreams—your vision of how the future will look with your goals completed.

- *Focus your attention on finding solutions.* Don't allow your attention to drift onto the suffering (the anxiety, aggravation, worry, or frustration) that results from what seem to be problems. Your problems are gifts, because they give you your greatest access to progress!

- *Find things for which to be grateful.* Make this one of your highest priorities. Set a target to write down ten new things you are grateful for today, and keep doing this every day. "Until when?" you ask? My reply: "Did I say there was a finish date?"

- *Know thyself.* Identify where and how you can do better. Learn about your strengths and weaknesses.

- *Knowing is not enough.* Keep taking actions that challenge you. Be intentional in your pursuit of continuous improvement. Keep a list of the improvements you are working on (such as sustained happiness and love).

If you have implemented most or all of these activities, you are well on track to achieving the goal of consistent happiness and love. Now it's time to go further, to find gold.

Love and Happiness As States of Being

Love and happiness that endure are the results of states of being rather than reactions to circumstances. We probably all know people who are far ahead of us in consistently radiating happiness and love. Their inner states of mind—their beings—*are* happiness and love. How can we go forward from being reactive, habitually anxious or angry, or just not quite satisfied enough to becoming more like these seemingly saintly individuals?

Are Happiness and Love What You Want?

Moving towards happiness and love as states of being begins with a decision about whether you are committed to achieving them. As with any goal, trying and then stopping when adversity or difficulties step in has no place if you really want—no, are *determined*—to be a person who is a beacon of love and happiness.

Why would you want anything less? These are the qualities that contribute massively to ourselves, to those closest to us, and to humanity as a whole. They make the path to other successes so much easier. Happiness and love attract to us exactly what it is that we most need and want.

There is nothing wrong with pursuing great goals, whether they be financial goals, career goals, family goals, or anything else. But do not expect them to be your source of happiness and love. Put your heart and mind in the right place, and these other goals will be yours anyway. We are now going to learn how to do this. It involves your connection with your Higher Self, or perhaps your *highest* self.

Manage Your Vibration and Thus Your Connection With Your Higher Self

In the last section I emphasized that happiness and love attract to us exactly what it is that we most need and what we most want. Understanding why this is so could, and I hope will, provide you with the motivation to make this state of mind, this vibratory signal, your highest priority.

Feeling happiness and love with no background issues or concerns means we have no resistances operating. We are holding and radiating a pure signal that gives generously to all levels of consciousness—humanity's collective consciousness, the subhuman consciousness of nature, and levels of consciousness that are higher, perhaps infinitely higher, than human consciousness. By radiating happiness and love, we are attracting circumstances and people with the same vibratory pattern, and we are attracting intuitions from supra-human levels—from our Higher Selves.

When you consistently link the goals, projects, and things that you desire with this energy, and continue to act to manifest those goals, success is guaranteed. But note the word *consistently* here. If you give mixed messages to subconsciousness, you will get mixed results. Thus, if you frequently experience frustration, impatience, or other negative feelings during the manifestation process, these are what you are attracting back. The way to link happiness and love to your projects is to maintain every day a clear vision of the dreams you intend bringing to fruition. This is the key to success. Feel the excitement and satisfaction of what you see that you will have accomplished in the future; see what you will be doing when your fabulous goal or goals have been achieved.

Where does your Higher Self (or highest self) figure in all this? The concept of a Higher Self is only useful if you find it useful. It makes perfect sense to me, empowering me and calling me forward to better, higher aspirations and performance. I believe in levels of consciousness beyond human awareness and comprehension, the range of which extends to infinitely fine levels of vibration. They are part of us; they are part of everything. We are connected to them just as we are connected in a vibratory manner to all the universe. However, if this is just "whoo-whoo" stuff from your viewpoint, that's fine. Don't engage with it. Just focus on the real gold here— make sure that every day and every hour of every day you make happiness and love your usual, resident vibration. Use this energy to promote the highest good. Look for ways to create exactly that.

I will be looking again at maintaining the connection with your Higher Self or best self in chapter 23.

Summary

1. Don't tolerate unhelpful emotions and behaviours playing out through you. Manage them right out of your repertoire. Many ways to go about this are discussed in this and other chapters.

2. Living with purpose and intentionality takes us a long way towards having sustained happiness and love. The Seven Steps list in this chapter is a great place to start.

3. Many people experience happiness and love in response to favourable events or certain people. However, when you rely on external circumstances or other people being aligned with your desires to activate your experience of happiness and love, these feelings will not last: they have been generated as transient subconscious reactions.

4. Having sustained happiness and love is only possible when it is consciously generated, regardless of circumstances and people. In other words, we must make it an automatic part of who we are; we must set it up as our resident way of being.

5. The journey to having sustained happiness and love starts with the commitment to achieving it.

6. The more successful we are in maintaining these feelings, regardless of circumstances, the more we are contributing to life as a whole and the more we are attracting even more happiness, love, and success to ourselves.

7. Holding the feelings of love and happiness as we visualize the completion of our goals, and the benefits from doing so, attracts their successful completion. Holding unhelpful thoughts and emotions as we tackle our goals merely attracts more of the same. Instead, see difficulties as gifts that hold the key to even more progress and happiness. This is an important habit to develop.

8. I believe that in keeping ourselves in a state of happiness and love, we are building a link with our Highest Selves that is ever stronger, ever more transparent, and ever freer of resistances, enabling it to express ever more easily through us.

Practice

1. Schedule time to spend following all the suggestions in the table "Managing Unhelpful Emotional Patterns."

2. Schedule time to spend working through the practices in the table "Seven Steps to Happiness and Love." Many of these were in the Practice sections of other chapters, and if you have completed that homework, you may well have little work to do here. Regardless, put new intentionality into getting these tasks completed to the best of your ability. It really is worth it for those who are determined to have a permanent breakthrough in being completely happy and permanently motivated by love.

3. When unhelpful emotions or behaviours occur, despite your best efforts, make a note in your What-I'm-Improving diary or file. This is the best way to learn from the experience.

    - Record the date, the circumstances, and how you reacted.

    - Identify what got in the way of your best self being expressed there.

    - What could you have done that would have been better?

4. Make having sustained happiness and love a goal. Go back to chapter 15 and follow the process of setting up and managing this goal.

    If you are tempted to skip this step:

    - Write down now what you remember about the benefits of sustained happiness and love.

    - Re-read the section, "Manage Your Vibration and Thus Your Connection with Your Higher Self." Read the summary again as well. Do this two or three times.

    - Also, keep this next fact in mind: simply knowing is the booby prize. The real prize is only available to those who put knowledge into action.

CHAPTER 22

THE GIFT OF COMPASSION

> Love and compassion are necessities, not luxuries.
> Without them, humanity cannot survive.
> —Dalai Lama XIV

> Until he extends the circle of his compassion to all living things, man will not himself find peace.
> —Albert Schweitzer

In this chapter we are moving on to a new and practical method of generating sustained happiness and love.

Compassion

This word is derived from the Latin word *misericordia,* meaning "tender-heartedness, pity, compassion, sympathy, and mercy." Empathy, open-heartedness, and caring are the key components, to my mind. Compassion says all this in a single word, and the experience of compassion automatically leads to love. Compassion is a quality that is highly valued in many religions (including Christianity and Buddhism), and yet one does not need any spiritual inclination to experience it.

The reason I am talking about compassion here is that practising it is probably the most successful way of creating happiness and love as your state of being. I have undertaken this practice myself and discovered new insights into and freedom from suffering, in relation to my own deep-seated issues. Practising being compassionate opens your heart and then your mind.

The practice that I followed, describe below and recommend to you, was inspired by chapter 8 of the book *The Lost Art of Compassion*, by Lorne Ladner, PhD[1]. I have taken the liberty of modifying what he wrote considerably. If you are interested in going more deeply into the subject of compassion, I definitely recommend his book to you.

A Practice to Develop Compassion

This compassion practice is not a one-off activity. It is an activity in which you will become more accomplished with practice. Daily practice is ideal. How long you spend doing it is up to you, but ten to fifteen minutes is reasonable.

Although there are six steps, it may help to start with just the first two or three. Extend the sessions if and when you are ready to include the others.

It is common for the intensity of compassion to fluctuate during this process. If you lose this feeling, simply go back to an aspect of life or a person or creature that makes generating compassion comes easily.

Never force the feeling. Don't judge yourself or feel bad about it if the feeling of compassion dries up. This is just a normal part of experience. I like the analogy of showering: do you judge yourself for how you feel during or after showering? Of course not. Handle the compassion practice in the same way: don't judge it. If it doesn't meet your expectations, just form the intention to start afresh the next day.

Step 1: Getting Started

Start by sitting down, relaxing, and focusing on your breath. The feeling of compassion is accompanied by slow, deep breathing. Set up this pattern of breathing now, and you have started the process.

Step 2: Find Compassion for Nature

Think about pets or animals in the wild that are suffering, seeing them in your mind. At the same time, hold the thought, *My heart goes out to them. May they be free of suffering.* You might remember beached whales, or dolphins that are caught in nets, or birds and animals kept in inhumane conditions. Send them your love whilst thinking, *My heart goes out to them. May they be free of suffering.*

Continue, with deep, steady breathing, your mind holding the key thought and your heart open with love and compassion. You may feel love and compassion radiating out from you and enveloping these creatures in need. Some people like to visualize this as a light that surrounds themselves and radiates out to the creatures they are holding in their minds. Continue this until you are ready to move on.

With your heart and mind now opened, you are ready to focus compassion on other areas of your choosing.

Step 3: Find Compassion for Yourself

- Now bring to mind any areas of your life where you have sadness, stress, anxiety, or pain.

- Hold the thought, *My heart is open. May I be free of suffering.* After doing this for a few minutes, you may notice a change in your feelings as you "get" this thought. Or you may just get it at a cognitive level.

- After a few minutes, bring to mind things that have caused you suffering. Notice your vulnerability. Engage with this step, seeing and experiencing things others have said or done, or that *you* have inadvertently said or done, that have brought suffering to you.

    The objective here is to engage the heart and open your feeling nature, but not to the point where you become so upset that you lose emotional control. It is important to intersperse the imagery and feelings with the thought, *My heart is open. May I be free of suffering.*

- Continue until you have developed the peace that accompanies finding compassion.

Step 4: Focus Your Compassion on Others.

Focus on people you love and the people to whom you are grateful.

Focus it on other people you know—work colleagues or people at your gym, for instance.

Focus it on particular groups such as your politicians and community leaders.

Think of the homeless and those in poverty in your country, and throughout the world.

With each person or group, hold them in mind as, with feeling and intentionality, you say to yourself the key thought:

> 'My heart goes out to them. May they be free of suffering.'

Step 5: Compassion for People Who Have Brought You Suffering

This step is only for people whose mental health is in good condition; it is not suitable for those who have experienced major psychological trauma. Focusing on those who have brought such suffering to your life may result in unhealed emotional wounds being opened. Search your heart, and if this is a possible or likely outcome, *do not proceed* with this step. You must see a counsellor before you embark on this step. I say this because there is no point in opening yourself to serious upset: the purpose of this compassion practice is healing, love, and happiness. No other outcome is acceptable; no risk of another outcome is worth taking. For those who have been through major psychological issues, step 5 is almost certainly a step too far.

If you are confident in your mental health, please read on. There is nothing in the process itself that is inherently dangerous.

The people to whom you ultimately want to bring your compassionate focus are those to whom you are averse, those who seem to be responsible for your past or present suffering. This might be your parents, your ex, your boss, or your neighbour, for instance. Pick one to start with.

- The first intentional thought to bring to mind as you focus upon them is this: *Just like me, these persons have suffering in their lives. Just like me, they are seeking happiness and love.*

  Hold on to these thoughts as you keep your attention on them.

- After a few minutes, change the thought to *My heart goes out to him/her/them. May they be free of suffering.*'

Note that feeling love and compassion for those you disapprove of does not mean you condone or in any way are altering your stance towards their behaviour. The effect of your love and compassion upon them is beyond your knowing, but as a positive force for good, it can do them no harm. There is always the possibility that it may start love resonating within them.

Concluding the Compassion Practice.

Decide when you are ready to finish. When you are, do the following:

- Review the scope of the creatures and people you have focussed upon, and renew your feeling of love and compassion for them.

- Focus once more on yourself and feel compassion for yourself. We are all far from perfection, and we need to be compassionate with ourselves as we learn and strive to improve.

- Form the intention to carry this compassionate strength with you as you proceed through this day and to bring it to mind when the going gets tough, when you are waiting, when you are busy, and when you see others suffering.

Note that when you see others suffering, you do not have to save or rescue them; they have their own learning process. Your compassion for them may be all that is appropriate. Staying true to your own goals is your first responsibility.

Compassion Or Judgement: Which Do You Choose?

Judging others whose actions or behaviours are selfish or unthinking is an automatic activity of our subconscious mind. This is true of all our negative reactions to others. However, this is unhelpful because it perpetuates separation between people; it feeds that separative principle in the human collective consciousness.

I recommend that you do not focus your attention on the negative deeds of others. Unfortunately, newspapers and TV news programmes love to put these before us. Focus instead on compassion for the suffering they have experienced or will experience, for this is an unavoidable consequence of their negative behaviour, even if they seem to get away with it.

Taking on Compassion As a Project

How does the compassion process relate to creating now? Taking on the compassion practice is a perfect example of the conscious mind creating an intention and an expectation. The subconscious mind responds to expectations; they are one of the main ways of training it. Your motivation to embark on this as a regular practice is the result of deciding that love and happiness are what you want. As you carry out the practice over time, subconsciousness learns to produce feelings of compassion, love, and happiness with increasing ease. Eventually, it learns to produce them automatically.

The results of regularly carrying out the compassion practice include greater connection with people, a greater ability to forgive, increased gratitude and appreciation for the gifts of life that were previously taken for granted, and the ability to remain happy and loving, independent of changing circumstances. This practice enables you to access the peace and love that are part of the underlying fabric of all life. This is a wonderful gift that will keep growing. This is a great project on which to embark.

Summary

1. I recommend using the compassion practice because carrying it out regularly has the ability to train the subconscious mind to bring you love and happiness automatically, as your usual way of being.

2. When your greatest being is generated in this way, you are freed up to choose your "doing" and not only to be more effective doing what you do but also to have more happiness and satisfaction while you do it. The actions that are motivated by the reactions of our less developed, junior autopilots start to disappear.

3. When love, compassion, and happiness are who you are, other resistances melt away. Your ability to achieve success in every area of life is greatly increased because you can focus, with far less distraction, on what you want. What you focus on expands, and as a result, solutions and opportunities open before you. This is the path to manifesting your heart's desire and the life of your dreams.

Practice

1. Decide when you will do your first compassion exercise.

2. Decide how long you want to spend on the first session.

3. After that, decide when and how long you will spend on the subsequent three sessions.

4. Create a weekly schedule showing the times when you will practise the compassion exercise. Daily practice is ideal.

5. Be sure to carry compassion with you always, and allow it to express through you as you go about your day.

Reference

1. Ladner, L. (2004). *The Lost Art of Compassion*. New York: HarperCollins Publishers.

CHAPTER 23

QUALITY OF SERVICE

> The best way to find yourself is to lose
> yourself in the service of others.
> —Mahatma Gandhi

Although every chapter in this book has been designed to help you develop creative thinking and insightful living, it has also been about improving your quality of service. As we conclude this book I want to draw your attention to matters that I think are the most important in relation to these three key areas.

Separation and Connection

It makes sense that when the conscious and the subconscious parts of the mind are working in a separate or even a partially coordinated fashion, the results will be less effective and less productive than if they work together in an integrated, cohesive way. Separation between these functional components has a negative impact on many aspects of life.

We live in and are a part of a universe, and connection or connectedness is one of its underlying characteristics. However, human beings tend to perceive separation from their neighbours, from other races, and even from the people in other cities in their own country. We feel separate from nature, despite the fact that the lives and achievements of every person that has ever lived have depended almost totally on nature. It has supplied the food we have all eaten, the water we have drunk and washed in, as well as the multitude of other products that have protected us from the elements and brought us into today's ways of living. The abundance of nature's gifts is extraordinary… and humbling. What service could we give and do in return to the many aspects of nature?

The point I want to get across is that redirecting our awareness towards recognizing what we are connected to has far more to offer than persisting with humanity's habitual focus on separation. Here is some homework for you. Start a list of all the things to which you are connected and build on this over the course of a month. During this month, list the benefits you see from concentrating on connection rather than separation. Think also about how we can guide people away from being separation-seekers and towards being connection-seekers.

Leadership

What brings people together is a common purpose—a common vision. A vision of what is possible doesn't just arrive; it is generated by individuals and grows because actions consistent with the vision are identified and then taken. Leadership is an important way of bringing people together.

Great orchestra conductors are great leaders. They aspire to a vision—albeit an auditory one—of the heights of mastery and beauty that are possible from the musical score before them. They identify the players who need assistance to achieve the high standard required. They ask for what they need, and together, the conductor and the orchestra practise until the performance has been brought as close to perfection as possible. Both parties are so determined to succeed that discipline is rarely an issue amongst these musical professionals.

It is possible for the components of the mind to work in exactly the same way. However, for many people, the conscious and subconscious parts of the mind are less developed in working seamlessly together. The more separated they are in their functioning, the more time and effort will be needed to manage problems. Also, progress in many aspects of life will be slower. The solution is to pay ongoing attention to the performance of your conscious mind, which is tasked with the responsibility of identifying and gently correcting unhelpful beliefs and junior autopilot behaviour. These have been discussed throughout the book.

Continue to Improve Your Creating-Now Ability

What frontiers of success do you want to explore and conquer? If you are interested in having a life that is great, right till the end, it makes sense to keep pushing the boundaries, aiming higher or in new directions. To do this, it is important to align yourself with the principle of continuous improvement. To maintain continuous improvement, you must keep developing your mind.

If you want to move progressively forward, the conscious mind, like a conductor, must lead the way, managing both aspects of the mind. I recommend the following process, which involves keeping a written record:

- Decide on the vision of what you want your life to look like. Review this at least once a month and change the details when appropriate.

- Identify your strengths and weaknesses in what you do consciously and in your automatic thoughts and emotional responses.

- Identify what you want to improve and the practices that are needed to develop the required habits and skills.

- Target mediocrity, and target whatever has become your new stage of "usual." Work out creative ways to improve everything that fits in these two categories, whether it be at home, in your fitness, in your environment, or at work, for example.

- Identify and track your successes. The little ones are just as important as the big ones. Feel the thrill of *all* your successes. They keep giving you the enthusiasm to strive for more and for better.

Commit to being sufficiently disciplined to take action in these areas on a regular basis—preferably every day. If you do this, the practices will become habits that will take you forward to consistent success, satisfaction, and happiness.

New Habits, New Skills

In time, all habits become outmoded. Good habits can take you so far, but then a new plateau is reached. To keep moving forward, you need new skills. With the vision of what you *now* want in place, you implement new habits that result in the skills that allow you to move forward again.

Make sure your conscious mind keeps refining its vision, keeps monitoring whether you are on track, and keeps looking at how it can improve your performance; this is what we are aiming to achieve in this book. Listen to the orchestra of your subconscious mind; see where improvements can be made and provide the conditions that enable subconsciousness to extend its powers. These are special skills that the conscious mind must learn.

Stage-Manage Your Success

In chapter 4 and particularly in chapter 21, we talked about the vibratory nature of everything. In relation to the functioning of the mind, what vibrates there are our thoughts and our feelings. We also said that the law of attraction is activated by the vibrations of our thoughts and feelings. Now, we want to attract people and circumstances that make us happy and bring us closer to success, don't we? It makes perfect sense, then, that if we aspire to become better in some way than we are now, we need to manage our thoughts and feelings as if we are already that much better or more successful and do the things that sort of person would do. If we do the opposite and hold on to the thoughts and feelings of *not* having what we want, that is exactly what we are attracting.

Have you decided what you want to change and improve? You may want to be happier, more confident, or wealthier. Or you may want to be a lawyer, sell real estate, or be someone who makes a difference in the world through another particular type of service. Once you have identified how you want to change, everything you think, say, feel and do is either bringing you towards or away from that.

I completed a stage-performance training course recently, and the presenters made this last point by saying that to be an amazing performer, you *must* be that particular amazing performer twenty-four hours a day. You cannot just be amazing only while you are on stage. "All the world's a stage," wrote William Shakespeare. Now I understand why he said that; it's profound. Let me explain why.

This example of training to be an amazing stage performer or presenter is a perfect analogy for training in any aspect of life. When "all the world's a stage," there is no part of the stage you can afford to miss out on; you must be amazing in every aspect and in every corner of your life, not just in centre stage (the area of your main desires). This quote also shows us that there is no time when you are not on stage. You must be the person you want to be twenty-four hours a day.

The strength of your desire is your most powerful motivator, helping you consistently maintain the vibration of the person you want to become. It is also the factor that will determine whether you achieve your goals.

There is ample guidance in the pages of this book to enable you to manage your vibration and the actions appropriate for creating the new you. I created this book to be an extraordinary resource for personal transformation. If you use it conscientiously, you could achieve complete enlightenment, if that is what you want, because the knowledge and skills from doing the practices will enable you to attract the teachers and all the other resources you need to take you there. The information and practices in this book will give you the knowledge and the means to train yourself to be, to do, and to have in any area of your choosing. This is what you deserve. This is what is possible.

Hone Your Instrument

You may recall that "Honing the Power of Your Mind" is the title of chapter 17. However, the principle of continuous improvement is so important that I want to mention an extra aspect here. It involves service and thus is linked to the quote at the start of this chapter.

We can think of ourselves as instruments or vehicles for improving the world in some small or large way. The magnitude of the mark we make on the world is determined by the size of our vision and the intensity of our desire to manifest it. I firmly believe that we were born to hone these instruments we each inhabit. We do so by being in service in the areas that call to us, whether they are inside our home or outside it, or whether through a sport, through manual labour, or through a particular industry.

Whatever your life looks like now and at any time in the future, expect change; expect problems. All change is an opportunity to hone your instrument—particularly the conscious and subconscious parts of your mind, because they control every other part of your instrument and the life it experiences. All change is also an opportunity to refocus on how you well you are providing service; on how and where improvements could be made. Monitoring the quality of service you give to others, and to yourself, is invaluable in creating a life of extraordinary success and satisfaction.

The Guidance of Your Higher Self

I have mentioned your Higher Self and your Highest Self previously. Whether you are spiritually inclined and prefer to capitalize the two words in those terms is up to you. Let's not have spirituality get in the way here. Let's just agree that there is a part of all of us that has immense access to beauty, strength, and beneficence; and beyond that, wisdom, understanding, and the limitless possibilities that exist for us individually and as a species. There are times when we see or feel a glimpse of that. I suspect our best access to it is when we experience our most special memories, those golden moments I mentioned at the end of chapter 13. Sustained happiness and love make us clearer channels for this highest part of ourselves to express through us, as I explained in chapter 21.

Take a minute or two right now to check your list of golden moments, and connect with the images and feelings of one or two of them. Close your eyes and allow yourself to be immersed in the depth of power, the richness of living, and the immensity of love. Generate the full expression of those feelings within yourself. This is so powerful, isn't it? You have access to this limitless powerhouse any time.

That's one aspect of connecting with your Higher Self. The other aspect needs a little thought. The next two sentences are the key. When you are experiencing fabulous, positive power within yourself, you are closely aligned with your Higher Self. When you are disempowered, that connection has been lost.

Now, we all have busy lives to lead. There just isn't time to take our eye off what we have to do in order to keep repeatedly plugging into our Higher Selves, even if we could remember to keep doing it! That's the kind of story your junior autopilot will come up with— that less mature, more childlike part of your subconsciousness that is desperate to have control and to survive.

You may remember that in chapter 11 we discussed identifying and managing the mind chatter that our junior autopilot constantly generates. It is important to know how to switch this off, because if you allow your attention to remain with the negativity it thrives on, you are allowing more and more negativity into your life. In chapter 11, I gave you to a quick way to politely dismiss this autopilot by doing brief mini-meditations: empty your mind of everything except your intention, your commitment, to centering yourself. Put your focus on your breath, your body, and the sounds around you. Do this for thirty to sixty seconds. You can probably accomplish it in the space of one or two full, deep breaths by applying real intention!

Once you are centred, aspire to be connected to your Higher Self. Generate those feelings either spontaneously (when you are well practised) or by connecting with one of your golden moment memories. You are now managing your vibration. You are now empowered, happy, and in a state of love, which connects you with the life force that vitalizes all forms of life. You have taken a few moments to hone your instrument. You are in a position to ask and answer the question "What is the most effective, most important thing for me to do right now?" It may surprise you to find it has nothing to do with the worry or stressful item you disengaged from moments earlier.

This sounds easy, and it is easy, if you make it a regular practice. Here is a summary in the following table.

> **Reconnecting with Your Highest Self Quickly**
>
> - Immediately recognize when you start feeling overwhelmed, upset, frustrated, confused, angry, tired, or any of the myriad of ways we feel when we have lost our Higher Self connection.
>
> - Realize that drift has occurred—your junior autopilot has gotten into the driving seat!
>
> - You have recognized what has happened, so your self-conscious mind is now back in charge. Now you can use the next part of the process:
>
>   - Put all other thoughts out of your mind except your commitment to living from the Highest and to being present to the sensations of your breath and your body.
>
>   - Do this for as long as it takes. You will know when you have reconnected with your Higher Self when love, happiness, and empowerment are back. There are no traces of unhelpful feelings.

Whether or not you start doing this now and whether you remember to keep doing it is entirely your choice. You need to be organized if you are going to make this and stage-managing your success part of your routine. Work with the organizing suggestions in chapter 13. Being intentional and organized will enable you to embed these practices and the many other life-skill practices presented in this book. They will take you exactly where you want to go.

The New, Exciting Journey Ahead

Teaching you how to achieve balanced cooperation between the conscious and subconscious parts of your mind has been one of main purposes for setting out the information and activities presented in this book. This won't have been achieved in a single reading. The job now is to start putting the knowledge into action. As I have said before, taking baby steps is the best way forward.

As the weeks and months go by, what is possible for you will increase, and it will amaze you. What will be possible for you in two, five, or ten years' time? If you continue to carry out the practices involved in managing yourself, the possibilities are limitless.

Create every moment of now purposefully with imagination and a light heart, and you will be on your way to a lifetime more fabulous than you can presently imagine.

Godspeed on your exciting journey!

Summary

1. The sense that we feel of separation from other people, from nature, and between many of the parts of our own lives is an illusion. Developing your sense of connection may take time, but the more you focus on this, the more you will experience the enormous benefits available from this practice.

2. The conscious and the subconscious parts of the mind can be trained to work seamlessly together. The more integrated they are, the more efficient and effective you become. The conscious mind, like a conductor, must lead the way. This book is dedicated to helping you achieve their harmonious, cooperative functioning.

3. Make continuous improvement one of your highest priorities. Apply this principle to every aspect of your life. Apply it to your vision, your dreams about what you are creating. Manage,

instead of reacting to, internal and external issues that seem to get in your way.

4. When you have identified what you want, everything you think, say, feel, and do is either bringing you towards or away from that. Manage your vibration so it resonates with happiness and love. This has fabulous benefits; be sure you know what they are.

5. You are a vehicle for improving the world in a variety of ways. This book is about honing your instrument so you can not only improve your own life but also provide ever better service in your interactions with others.

6. When we are experiencing happiness and love, we are clearer channels for our Highest Selves to express through us, providing us with solutions, inspiration and opportunities. Use the opportunities presented in chapters 21–23 to strengthen your access to this valuable asset.

7. Your creating-now potential is limitless. Your creating-now *abilities* depend on your ability to manage the conscious and subconscious parts of your mind. Be in action. Keep improving these self-management skills and your creating abilities are absolutely certain to overtake your current potential!

Practice

1. Connection versus Separation

    - Start listing of all the things to which you are connected. Build on this list every week.

    - List the benefits you see from focusing on connection rather than separation.

- How can we guide people towards being connection-seekers?

- Spend time deciding which connections you want to make stronger and make ongoing contributions to.

2. Fan the flame of your desires and pay attention to them. Desire is your most powerful self-motivator, and it is the factor that determines whether you achieve your goals.

    - Be enthusiastic and excited about everything!

    - Be curious; make learning and improving some of your main values. Use the energy of new understanding to propel you forward.

    - *You* are the power station of energy for your life!

3. Ask yourself this important question when things start going wrong or when you wish you were somewhere or with someone else: "Is what I am thinking and feeling bringing me towards or taking me away from being the person I want to be?"

4. Ask yourself this question when you feel unmotivated or disempowered: "Am I willing to tolerate feeling like this, or am I going for gold, prepared to take all the actions needed to take home the prize I'm after?"

    Getting gold is the result of being in action.

ABOUT THE AUTHOR

Adrian Harrison was born in Nottingham, England, but grew up in Adelaide, where he graduated in medicine. After several years of post-graduate training in respiratory medicine in Adelaide, Sydney and Los Angeles, he took up a Specialist post in Auckland. For more than thirty years he has enjoyed a successful career as a Specialist Chest Physician in hospital and private practice.

Adrian had no interest in personal development until the late 1980's when an unexpected major life event—divorce—suddenly turned his world upside down. He began looking at his own life differently, and discovered a number of completely new interests. He found himself at home with Qabalah, which opened a wealth of information about Divinity and mankind. He also acquired a passionate interest in what makes people tick: how we think, and how and what we create. Beneath the complexity of people's individuality he learned that human beings share many characteristics, including the potential to be exceptional. He realised that everyone is capable of making amazing contributions to humanity, both locally and globally. Discovering how to unlock people's creative and caring talents, understanding the mind-set required to achieve extraordinary success and related topics have occupied his reading (along with medical journals) since about 1990. Over the years he completed a number of personal development courses, motivated by a desire to become the best he could be, especially in terms of being open- hearted, open-minded, whilst also being focused and purposeful.

Adrian has published more than 30 medical research articles, topic reviews and management guidelines. He has been a Medical School lecturer and helped junior colleagues become successful Specialists. Besides focusing on excellence in the medical aspects of patient care, for at least the last 15 years his physician role has also included motivating people to self-manage their health. Smoking cessation is an obvious example. Sometimes he found helping people to stop smoking straight forward, but more often it required gentle and yet sometimes firm persistence and being willing to support those people in doing *whatever it takes* to quit. Whilst this required him to show leadership, guiding people towards their strengths, Adrian was acutely aware that the choices made by his patients were always to be respected. Like others, Adrian has observed that nicotine addiction doesn't occur in isolation. He feels privileged that so many smokers have been willing to unlock the secret fears and pains they have numbed by smoking, allowing him the opportunity to help them see these issues in a more positive and often a less significant light.

Becoming a Life Coach was a natural progression of all this activity inside and outside medicine. In the last few years Adrian has had many life coaching clients. He has found that a detective-like approach to sorting out personal issues has parallels with the diagnostic approach for medical problems. Life coaching and developing self-improvement tools and techniques are his new career. The challenge for Adrian now is to excel even more in contributing to people's quality of life as a Life Coach than he achieved as a Chest Physician. This is definitely his intention.

Adrian's principal coaching niche is busy professional people - in particular, Doctors, Lawyers and Executives. However, he is also available to clients involved in other disciplines. His coaching curriculum covers many areas of life. A principle aim is to help clients bring the wealth of information stored in the subconscious mind out into conscious awareness, where it can be managed and improved. Spirituality is not included unless specifically requested.

Adrian is also certified in, and licensed as a High Performance Coach. This course is eminently suited for people who are very motivated to develop every aspect of themselves and go well beyond their current potential.

We invite you to check out Adrian Harrison's website, https://www.SpinDoctor.com and to email him at adrian@spindoctor.com

---

BONUS OFFER for book readers:

To obtain free training and tools,
go to www.spindoctor.com/bookbonustraining.

Add the the code BOOKBONUS
to access your free gift.

INDEX

Act "As if," 91-92, 238
Acknowledging
    qualities you share with others, 271
    successes, 176
    your courage, 238
Adaptation, the movie (quote), 76
Addiction, 41, 310
Affirmations
    are not enough, 50, 107
    about commitments, intentions 70, 73-74, 248
    for managing goals, 201
    for managing sense of lack, 74
    how to modify them, 107-108
    see also Fears
All Blacks, 208
Allen, James (quote), 179
Allowing
    problems to exist vrs resisting, 160
    your dreams to develop, 184
    see also How; Open

Appearance, 240
Attention, 27-29, 31, 32-33, 61-64
    anchored, 63, 90, 227, 264
    autopilot switching it on, 32-33
    free, 44, 63, 83
    give all or none, 70, 71, 143, 222
    leaking, 62, 65, 70
    meditation and, 33, 137-138
Australian Lung Foundation (slogan), 210
Autopilot, 29, 34, 37-45, 49, 64, 66, 68
    cost of being on, 40-41
    procrastination and, 117
    see also Comfort zone; Imagination and roadblocks to using it; Junior autopilot

Baby steps,
    applying knowledge and, 306
    becoming your best and, 236
    exiting the comfort
        zone and, 131
    intentions and, 73
Balanced or integrated life: see Roles
Beliefs, 102-114
    core, 103
    definition, 24
    emotions and, 81, 83, 88
    experiences and, 78, 104
    list of, 112, 113
    managing disempowering
        beliefs, 110-111
    memory and, 103
    personality and, 103-104
    reality and, 23-24, 113
    revealing technique, 109-110
    storehouse of, 30, 32
    truths and, 24, 102-103, 112
    see also Fears
Being
    who you are 230-232
    being happiness and love,
        274, 284-285
    being love and
        compassion, 242
    choosing, in the face of
        difficulty, 232
    examples, 238, 247
    in action, 115, 308
    mindset, 237
    when driving, 240, 247
    when striving, 226
    vs doing mode, 226, 236-238

Being present, see Living in the now
Being your best, 238-246
    being a champion, 245
    in every situation, 243-245
    moving to higher ground, 256
    speech and, 241-242
    what is your very best?
        243-245
Blame, 53, 54, 56, 148, 153,
    160, 220, 230, 256, 272
Brainstorming, 92-93, 98,
    99, 197, 229, 267
Breathing, 210-212, 216
    airway resistance and,
        261-262
    anxiety and, 142, 211
    being present and, 45
    breath control practices, 216
    breathe into the pain, 156
    compassion exercise and, 291
    considered as a gift, 215
    disordered breathing
        pattern, 210-212
    getting back to sleep and, 276
    highly charged circumstances
        and, 142, 211, 212, 215
    meditation and, 57, 58, 137-
        138, 213, 304, 305
    sensations, 45, 156
    see also Suffering
Brown, Michael, author: *The
    Presence Process*, 159, 161
Buddha (quote), 27
Build on your successes,
    132, 165-166, 176
    success diary and, 176

Burchard, Brendon, author: *The Charge: activating the 10 human drives that make you feel more alive*, 231, 234

Castellano, Rich, author: *The Smile Prescription*, 247, 249

Change
    force for, 54
    habits, 30
    make changes gradually, 97, 127-128, 130, 131
    needing to, 125-126
    reality, 25
    time for, 72
    suffering as an initiator of, 158
    yourself, not others, 83-85, 129
    see also Baby steps;

Challenge
    habit of challenging yourself, 131
    yourself as a communicator, 145
    yourself to create the best, 245
    yourself to do better, 126
    see also Being extra-ordinary

Choices, choosing,
    choosing a being, 238
    choosing a goal, 193
    choosing vs trying, 236
    don't let your habit mind choose for you, 266
    during communication, 141-142
    feelings, 67, 81
    free attention and, 63
    love and happiness and, 86, 88
    self-conscious mind and, 30, 34
    thoughts, 81
    trying and, 236
    what you allow into your mind, 159, 220-222, 231
    see also Being, who you are

Chopra, Deepak (quote), 36
Churchill, Winston (quote), 218
Clooney, George (quote), 250
Collective consciousness, 51-54, 76
    changing, influencing it for good, 52-54, 86, 246, 285
    separative principle in, 294
    upsets and, 252
    see also Pain body

Comfort zone, 122-132
    characteristics of, 122-123
    payoff and cost, 124
    procrastination and, 116
    resisting and, 264
    signs of living in, 124-125
    subconscious mind and, 127
    see also Change;

Communication, 133-146
    judgement and, 135
    language rules and accuracy, 139-140
    listening, 134-136
    non-verbal, 139
    speaking, 139-142

unspoken, 135
see also Music; Speech habits; Words
Compassion, 289-296
   benefits of the compassion practice, 295
   components of, 289
   driving and, 247
   gives access to lasting happiness and love, 289, 290
   practice (six steps), 290-294
   world as a mirror and, 257
Conductor and orchestra, 31-32, 298-299
Confucius (quote attributed to), 235
Connection
   mind-body, 269, 276, 207-217
   separation and, 297-298
   with your highest, 267, 278, 305
Consciousness
   fluidic nature, 51, 224
Continuous improvement, 168, 283, 299, 302, 306
Cooley, Mason (quote), 115
Covey, Stephen (quote), 89
Creating, 15, 16
   abilities, 33-34, 307
   beliefs and, 26
   with or without intention, 21
Creativity
   killing off with persistent toil, 93
   see also Imagination

Dalai Lama XIV (quote), 289
Davies, Ann (quote), 21
Design
   your life, 94-96
   your personality, 96-97
Desensitization to trauma, 159
Distractions,
   harnessing emotional power and, 82-83, 87
   preventing them from putting you off-course, 202
Doing mode, 236-237,
   body sensation awareness and, 208
   forcing and, 226
   vs being mode, 236-238
Dooley, Mike, author: *Leveraging the Universe and infinite Possibilities*, 219, 234
Dreams
   creative dreaming, 183-185
   see also Allowing
Driving, 65, 69, 154, 208, 236, 240, 247

Ego, 30, 37
   alter ego, 92
Emotions, 76-88
   awareness of, 45, 55
   changing from negative to positive, 81-82
   expectations and interpretation of the circumstances, 87
   harnessing emotional energy, 82-83, 87

music and, 142
primary, 105
quality of life and, 77-79, 87
subconscious mind and,
    30, 39, 74, 251
Emotional upsets
    beliefs and, 114
    causes, 250
    interrupt before reacting with,
        150, 160-161, 254-255
    junior autopilot thoughts
        and, 253-254
    learning from, 256-258
    managing, 253-256
    move to higher ground,
        255-256
    prevention by planning
        and practising, 260
    putting an end to, 258-259
    see also Collective consciousness;
        Impartial observer;
        Law of attraction;
Emotional triggers
    identifying, 158, 259
    'pain body' and, 251
Emotional mire, extracting
    yourself from, 264-267
Energy
    generating more, 230-231
    resisting and, 253, 264, 276
    success and, 285
    thoughts and, 218-219
    trapped, 277, 278
Enlightenment, 16, 302
Expectations, 65-66
    emotions and, 80, 87

from the compassion
    practice, 295
meditation and, 57
subconscious mind and,
    31, 33, 65-66, 295
unmet, 65, 250, 259
values and, 189
Einstein, Albert (quote), 47
    equation, 47

Fears, 105-110, 113-114
    procrastination and, 117
    values and, 190
Focusing ability
    education and, 28
    meditation and, 33,
        43, 138, 220
    self-conscious mind and,
        28, 29, 61, 237
    ways to maintain, 64, 71-73
Forcing
    failure risk and, 132
    forcing vs striving, 226, 232
Ford, Henry (quotes), 104, 131

Getting what you want
    resonate with the feeling of
        having it, 85, 307
Gandhi, Mahatma (quote), 297
Goals,
    alignment and, 50
    benefits, 203
    goal setting, 126, 193-198
    managing, 118, 166, 198-202
    outcomes, 172

requirements for achieving, 50, 203, 204
staying true to your, 294
values and, 191
see also Choosing; How; Mind mapping
Golden goose (analogy for the body), 168, 212
golden goose care, 71-72, 94, 212, 216,
Goldman, Burt, 92, 101

Happiness
and free attention, 42, 63-64
effects on the body, 107
freedom from resistances and, 264, 275-276
intention and, 22, 77, 85
make it your top priority, 154
news and, 220-221
practise it, as a state of mind, 85
that lasts, 85, 88, 280-288
the secret to, 85
thoughts and, 219, 264
see also Compassion, Love; Resistance
Healing the past, 159, 161
Herold, Thomas, 62, 75
High performance, 130, 132, 311
see also Being extra-ordinary
Higher Self, 67, 151, 285-288
connecting with, 285-287, 303-305
guidance of, 303-305
Highest good, 242, 286

Hill, Napoleon, author: *Think and Grow* Rich, 91, 101
How
let the universe manage the, 183

Ideal day off, 186
Ideal work day, 186
Imagination, 89-100
staying present and, 43
beliefs and, 104
benefits of using, 30, 185, 306
how to free it up, 91-93
roadblocks to using it, 90
subconscious mind and, 30
and managing unhelpful emotional patterns, 281
See also Thinking
Impartial observer, 41, 254-255, 258, 259
Inertia, 30
Inner commentator, 136-137
See also Mind chatter
Intention, 48-51, 61, 64-66, 73
create supports for your intentions, 225
emotional reactions and, 67, 70, 77
meditation, 57, 138
nurturing, 137
procrastination and, 115, 117
sustained vision and, 50
training your subconscious mind and, 69, 144
the person who gets things done, 119

see also Expectations,
    Open; Problems
Iyengar, B.K.S (quote), 207
Judgements
    beliefs and, 23
    communication and, 135, 241
    creates separation, 294
    habit, 257, 294
    lapse of self-discipline
        and, 132
    learning and, 79, 87
    meditation and, 57
    negative emotions and, 88
    limited perspective and, 241
    self-, 79
    subconscious mind and,
        39, 136, 294
    see also Impartial observer
Junior autopilot/'Junior', 37-39
    conscious and creative powers
        displaced by, 43
    correcting behaviours it
        generates, 296, 299
    dismissing, in meditation,
        303-305
    five characteristics, 38-39
    modified by practising
        compassion, 295, 296
    pride and, 50
    worries and, 39, 40
    see also Emotional upsets

Know thyself, 283
Knowing is the booby prize, 17, 288

Ladner, Lorne (author): *The Lost
    Art of Compassion*, 290, 296
Late presentation with illness
    symptoms, 209
Law of attraction, 48-51
    attracting the best, 239, 241
    beliefs and, 113
    definition, 48, 49
    desires and, 85
    inner conflict, worries,
        fears and, 50, 106
    main elements of, 51
    thoughts and feelings and,
        48, 85, 106, 113, 254
    see also What you want
Leadership, 298-299
    Self-consciousness and,
        31-32, 33, 34, 299
Limitations
    beliefs and, 103-104, 111, 114
    breaking free of, 179-184
    learning about, 256-259
Lists
    as a memory aid, 224
    for managing upsets, 258
    monthly task list, 170,
        174-175, 178
    of beliefs that support
        you, 113
    of things you fear, 113
    of goals, tasks, intentions
        and lessons learned,
        224, 225, 232-233
    of new possibilities, 186
    of things you are
        tolerating, 197

of uninvited thoughts, 74
of upset triggers, 150
of roles, 167-168, 174, 177, 197, 246
of things you need, 233
special memories, golden moments, 176-177, 200, 203, 303
success diary, 119, 175, 176, 281
weekly task list, 119-120, 121, 166, 170, 173-174
see also Ideal day off; Ideal work day; Roles; Three Key words

Living in the now, 36-45
body awareness and, 208-209
consequences of not being present, 40-41
features of not living in the now, 34
meditation and awareness of now, 213
opportunities from, 41-44
risk factors for not being present, 44-45
significance of now, 42-43, 44

Love
consciously generated, 282-286
developing your love nature, 86, 136-137,
happiness and, 86, 247, 282-288
see also Compassion; Happiness; Nurturing yourself; Seven steps to happiness and love

Love, Roger, author: *Set Your Voice Free*, 142, 146

Mapes, Richard, author: *Quantum Leap Thinking*, 192, 204
Mead, Rachael (quote) 165
Meaning of life, 22
Meditation
and mind chatter, 135-138, 143, 213, 304
benefits of, 214
details of, 56-58, 137-138, 212-214
heightened awareness and, 138, 213, 220
mini-meditations, 138, 304
training in being present, 210
training the mind and, 33-34, 137-138, 220
see also Transparency
Mediocrity, 123, 177, 300
Memory
managing, supporting 178, 224
role of the brain, 29
sub-conscious mind and, 23, 29, 61, 103, 112
see also Richard Mohs; Subconsciousness

Memories
    golden moments (special memories), 176-177, 200, 203, 303
Mind-body connection, 207-217
    being in the mind, 208-209, 215
    body sensations, 45, 156, 208-209
    pain trapped in the mind or body, 159
    posture, 208
    see also Choices; Late presentation of illnesses
Mind chatter, 135-138
    and meditation, 137-138
    self-critical internal chatterbox, 136-137, 149
    upsets and the internal chatterbox, 253
    See also Inner commentator; Meditation
Mind mapping 170-171
    example: Dave's first mind map, 194-195
    for roles and goals, 193-195
    problems, 228
Mistakes
    autopilot and, 30, 34, 79
    learn from them, 113, 132
    speaking and, 134
Monitor
    body sensations, 208-209
    performance of the conscious mind, 300
    service quality, 303
    thoughts, 219
    See also Success Diary
Motivation
    by love, 287, 295
    excitement, enthusiasm and, 165, 177
    generating more energy and drive, 192, 203, 230-231, 308
    intense desire and, 83, 130, 285, 302, 308
    purpose and, 274-275
    to become the best, 309
Mohs, Richard, 29,
Mother Teresa (quote), 147; 100, 158
Music
    in speech, 142, 144
    influence on the mind, 221
    piano music, 273
    to support intentions, 225

Nature, 298
    compassion for, 291
    desire, 83
    love, 86, 137
    separation from, connection with, 297, 306
    vibratory, 47-48, 221, 301
News, 221
Now *see* Living in the now
Negative thoughts
    are opportunities, 54

don't tolerate, 25, 81,
 87, 223, 283
eliminating their power,
 254-255
external sources of, 220-221
goals and, 196
identify and replace, 66,
 69-70, 81-82, 87,
 136-137, 265, 266
inner source, 136
Neurotransmitters
 and facial expression, 240
Nurturing yourself, 136, 137
 taking care of yourself, 154

Objectivity, 40, 43, 157, 256
 being present and, 226
 meditation and, 214

OneNote, 171
Open
 channel, 276, 279
 heart, 289, 310
 to abundance, 49, 74, 107,
  128, 132, 173, 182
 to new or limitless
  possibilities, 35, 52, 54,
  82, 90, 96, 111, 125, 153,
  173, 197, 227, 266, 303
Opportunities
 attracting, 93, 185,
  239, 296, 307
 from adversity or change,
  257, 302, 303
 from failures, 257, 271

from living in the now,
 41-42, 54, 64
from upsets and painful
 experiences, 25-26,
 129, 259, 282
from problems, 152, 226,
 227, 232, 233, 258
from success, 165, 177
from suffering, 54,
 157, 158, 160
look for, 97, 108, 125, 126,
 131, 172, 184, 258
procrastination and, 116, 117
see also Build on your
 successes
Organizing, organization
 balanced life and, 166
 being extra-ordinary and,
  129-130, 177, 178
 delegate or dismiss and, 171
 document everything, 202
 improving standards and, 171
 lack of, 165
 life, 166-175, 178
 time, 175-176
 procrastination and,
  117-120, 121
 see also Goals; Lists; Roles;
  What you want

Pain body, 251
 see also Emotional triggers
Personality types
 analogy with buildings, 37

Planning, 120, 172-173, 175,
    192, 201, 202, 203
Positives
    focusing on, 23, 24
    in suffering, 157-158
Present: *see* Living in the now
Pride, 50, 153
Problems, 226-230
    allowing, not resisting
        them, 160
    solving, 91-93,
    see also Imagination;
        Opportunities
Procrastination, 115-121
    causes and costs, 116-117, 124
    definition, 115
    potential procrastination
        items (PPIs), 117,
        119, 173, 174
Purpose, 271-275
    conflicting values and, 191
    creating with, 15, 21, 115
    living a life of, 22
    meditation, 57
    of life, 22, 63
    of life's painful episodes, 277
    of people and events, 271-274
    of your life, 274-275

Qabalah, 13, 77, 170, 309

Reality, 21, 23-25
    beliefs and, 23-24, 103-105
    breaking free of a
        limiting, 179-182
    fears and, 105
    future, 200
    words create, 242
Relationship
    between current and past
        suffering, 159
    between original and
        replacement
        thoughts, 81
    between the two parts of
        the mind, 31-32, 34
    see also Conductor
        and orchestra
Relaxation and rejuvenation,
    72, 93, 94, 175,
Resistance, 261-279
    avoiding and, 252-253, 259
    examples of inner, 276-277
    forcing and, 226
    four questions for freeing
        resistances, 267-268
    in the body during
        suffering, 156
    moving past, and finding
        solutions, 267-270, 278
    negative emotions
        and, 244, 259
    practice feeling free of,
        222, 275-276, 277,
        279, 287, 296
    procrastination and, 115
    signs pointing to, 255-257
    subconsciousness and, 30, 155
    to being organized, 166
    see also Comfort zone;
        Transparency, the power of

Roles 167-170, 174-175, 177
    and creating new ideas and
        possibilities, 186, 246
    creating beings and, 246
    goal setting and, 197
    mind maps for, 193-194
Role play, acting, 91-92, 150

Schweitzer, Albert (quote), 289
Self
    manage your sense of, 54, 160
    sense of, 30, 37, 38, 104
    worth, 53, 84
    see also Attention; Being;
        Focusing ability; Intention
Separation
    and connection 294-295,
        297-298, 306, 307-308
    between the conscious
        and sub-conscious
        minds, 297, 306
    see also Judgement
Service, 53-54, 132, 135,
    252, 275, 297-308
Seven steps to happiness
    and love, 283
Shakespeare, William (quote), 301
Shaw, George Bernard
    (quotes), 89, 133, 280
Smile, smiling, 208, 216, 247, 249
    see also Castellano, Rich
Smoking, 41, 71, 78, 124,
    235, 236, 310
Special memories, 176-177, 303
    visualizing and, 200, 203
    see also Lists

Speech, speaking, 139-146, 241-242
    habits, 140-142
    influences the future, 242
    language rules, 139
    music in, 142
    and being the best, 235-236
SpinDoctor.com, 311
    email invitation 91, 170,
        192, 203, 278, 311
Star Trek: Voyager (TV series)
    virtual doctor, 228, 251
Star Trek: The Borg (TV
    series) (quote), 261
Subconsciousness, sub-conscious
    part of the mind 29-31
    messengers from
        subconsciousness,
        68-69, 256-257
    responds to the predominant
        vibration, 50
    sabotage and, 17
    suffering and, 147
    training the, 32-34,
    see also Beliefs; Conductor
        and orchestra;
        Judgements; Memory;
        Mind chatter;
        Junior autopilot;
        Relationship; Self
Success
    build on your successes,
        159, 176
    stage manage, 301-302
Success diary, 176
    a key tool in managing
        life, 177

during personal development
time, 175
ending procrastination
and, 119
Suffering, 147-161
extreme, 154-157
focus on breathing, 156
is a call to action, 148-149
is not the enemy, 155, 227
learning from, 252, 256-258
lighten up, look at the
big picture, 154
managing, 23-24, 63, 68-69
positive aspects, 151-153
trapped pain, 159, 278
vision for good and, 49-50, 51
see also Change;
Resistance; Victim
Sylver, Marshall (exercises), 186

Taking it personally, 152-154,
see also Victim
Three key words, 67, 151
Thinking,
true thinking, 220, 231
Thought police, 25, 26, 27, 220
Thoughts
are just thoughts, 180, 255
become things, 219, 231
beliefs and, 23, 25-26
categories: helpful and
harmful, 219
do not define who you
are, 231, 266
don't tolerate negative, 25

good-bye, old thought, 266
have energy, 218
having, 135, 231, 253
identifying thoughts, 33, 304
limit their significance,
25, 231, 254, 255
origins, 30
reasons to monitor and
manage, 218-219
reality and, 25
replace, 25, 66, 81-82, 87, 266
self-critical, 136, 149
uninvited, 74
Tolle, Eckhart, author: *The Power
of Now*, 37, 46, 251
Training
practising compassion
trains the sub-
conscious mind, 295
your inner commentator,
136-137
see also Meditation
Transparency, the power of, 221-222
Trying, 235-236

Upsets: *see* Emotional upsets
Use the world as a mirror,
68-69, 70, 256-257

Values, 189-192
conflict between purpose
and values, 191
conflict between values
and fears, 190
core, 189, 191

identifying your values,
189-190
leadership and, 189-190
respect others' values, 192
staying true to, 84, 96
wishes and, 50
see also Three key words
Vibratory nature of everything,
47-48, 76, 301
human consciousness
and, 48, 51, 54
levels of consciousness
beyond human
awareness, 286
managing your vibration,
304-305
Victim
beliefs about, 82
changing from being a victim
of circumstances, 24,
82, 128-129, 148
doing mode and, 237
don't be a victim to
your subconscious
mind, 66-67, 69
eliminate victim thinking,
149-154
of suffering, 148, 160
stop being a victim of
negative thoughts
and feelings, 66-67,
69-70, 81-82, 253-256
Vision
board, 203-204, 225
of what you want, 54, 130, 299

leadership and, 298-299
sustained vision, 50
Visualizing
and achieving goals, 199-
200, 203, 287
during compassion
practice, 291
love descending, 84
yourself in a chosen
being, 246
see also Special memories

What you focus on expands,
62, 239, 276, 296
What you want
finding solutions and, 54, 92,
125, 128, 180, 255, 259
harnessing emotional
power and, 83, 87
high performance
and, 130, 230
intention or expectation
and, 65, 295
knowing and obtaining, 21
31, 56, 85, 88, 95, 96,
108, 114, 131, 172,
181-183, 186, 225, 276,
284, 296, 299-304
law of attraction and,
49, 85, 184
most, 83, 151-152, 188-204
see also Being extra-
ordinary; Change;
Dreams; Organization;
Suffering; Visualizing

Whiteboard, 118, 170, 171, 175, 178
Williams, Graham, PhD, author:
    Life in Balance: The Lifeflow Guide to Meditation, 214, 217
Words, 141-142, 144, 191, 241-242
    three key words, 67, 151

Worries, 222-224
    managing worry, 223
    origin, 39, 222

Zander, Rosamund and Benjamin, authors: *The Art of Possibility*, 37, 46

CPSIA information can be obtained
at www.ICGtesting.com
Printed in the USA
LVHW021300270720
661634LV00015B/578